William Watts Hart Davis

# The Fries Rebellion 1798-99

An Armed Resistance to the House Tax Law, Passed by Congress, July 9, 1798

William Watts Hart Davis

**The Fries Rebellion 1798-99**
*An Armed Resistance to the House Tax Law, Passed by Congress, July 9, 1798*

ISBN/EAN: 9783337207267

Printed in Europe, USA, Canada, Australia, Japan

Cover: Foto ©ninafisch / pixelio.de

More available books at **www.hansebooks.com**

# THE
# FRIES REBELLION

## 1798-99

AN ARMED RESISTANCE TO THE HOUSE TAX LAW, PASSED BY CONGRESS, JULY 9, 1798, IN BUCKS AND NORTHAMPTON COUNTIES, PENNSYLVANIA.

BY

## W. W. H. DAVIS, A. M.

AUTHOR OF "EL GRINGO, OR NEW MEXICO AND HER PEOPLE;" "HISTORY OF THE 104TH PENNSYLVANIA REGIMENT;" "LIFE OF GENERAL JOHN LACEY;" "HISTORY OF THE HART FAMILY; "THE SPANISH CONQUEST OF NEW MEXICO;" "THE HISTORY OF BUCKS COUNTY, PA.;" "LIFE OF JOHN DAVIS," AND "HISTORY OF THE DOYLESTOWN GUARDS."

DOYLESTOWN, PA.
1899.

Entered, According to Act of Congress, in the Year 1899, by
WILLIAM W. H. DAVIS,
In the Office of the Librarian of Congress, at Washington, D. C.

Doylestown Publishing Company, Prin
Doylestown, Penna.

# CONTENTS.

|  | PAGE |
|---|---|
| Title Page | 1 |
| Contents | 3 |
| Illustrations | 5 |
| Dedication | 7 |
| Preface | 10 |
| Chapter I. Cause of Rebellion, John Fries | 1 |
| " II. Insurgents Prepare to Resist the Law | 14 |
| " III. Fries Captures the Assessors | 25 |
| " IV. Opposition to House Tax Law in Northampton | 38 |
| " V. The Marshal Makes Arrests in Northampton, | 48 |
| " VI. Rescue of the Prisoners at Bethlehem | 57 |
| " VII. The President Issues his Proclamation | 67 |
| " VIII. Troops Called Out to Suppress the Insurrection | 75 |
| " IX. Rev. Charles Henry Helmuth Issues an Address | 87 |
| " X. The Army Marches from Quakertown to Allentown and Returns to Philadelphia via Reading | 102 |
| " XI. Trial of John Fries | 115 |
| " XII. Pardon of Fries | 129 |
| " XIII. Conclusion | 137 |
| Appendix | 1 |
| Index | 9 |

## ILLUSTRATIONS.

|   |   | PAGE |
|---|---|---|
| 1. | Frontispiece. W. W. H. Davis | |
| 2. | Threatening Notice | 12 |
| 3. | Sellers' Tavern | 26 |
|    | Erected About 1780. | |
| 4. | Old Friends Meeting House, Quakertown | 42 |
|    | Torn Down 1862. | |
| 5. | William Henry | 56 |
| 6. | Crown Inn, South Bethlehem | 74 |
| 7. | Old Lancaster House, Quakertown | 90 |
|    | Torn Down 1841. | |
| 8. | Bridge Over the Lehigh | 106 |
|    | Built About 1795. Torn Down 1817. | |
| 9. | Present Friends Meeting House, Quakertown | 124 |
| 10. | Sun Inn, Bethlehem | 140 |
|    | About 1791. | |

## Dedication.
This Volume is Dedicated to the Students of History.

# PREFACE.

In presenting this volume to the public, it seems meet and proper the circumstances, under which it was written and published, should be stated.

I purchased the Doylestown (Pa.) *Democrat* 1858, and, being interested in local history, began collecting the facts, relating to the armed resistance to the house-tax law of 1798, and writing it up for my paper. I had heard a good deal of it in my youth and was curious to know more. It had its birth in Milford township, Bucks county, Pa.; thence extending into the adjoining townships of Northampton, and, in unwritten history, was known as the "Milford Rebellion." There is no evidence that the people of Montgomery county had any part in it.

I visited the locality where Fries and his "insurgents," as they were called, operated; interviewed his son Daniel, his only surviving child, then an old man of over 70, and others who lived in that section at the time of the trouble, hunted up all the known records and examined the newspaper files of the period. By the winter of 1859-60 I had collected considerable material and published portions of it in my newspaper. Since then additional matter has been added to the text, and many new facts, pertinent to the subject, are embodied in foot notes.

Being satisfied the facts, relating to this interesting episode, would have been lost, had they not been collected when they were; and believing them of sufficient interest to be preserved in some more enduring way, then attaches to the columns of a weekly newspaper, I determined to publish them in book form. The manuscript was prepared for the press several years ago, but the publication was deferred, from time to time until the present, and it is now given to the public with some misgivings. The events narrated are not only interesting in themselves, but too suggestive of the friction between the people and their newly established government, to allow them to become lost to the student of history. I have several friends to thank, including Messrs. John W. Jordan,* Charles Broadhead, Bethlehem, and Ellwood Roberts, Norristown, in the matter of furnishing illustrations for the volume.

W. W. H. DAVIS.

*Doylestown, Pa., March 4, 1899.*

---

*Pennsylvania Historical Society.

# THREATENING LETTER.

The following is a translation of the threatening letter facing page 12, sent, by an insurgent, to Captain Jarrett, and is one of the earliest exhibitions of Kukluxism extant:

A sure warning (certain report) to you John Sheret if you have already advised the people who are for liberty that they should not go armed to Bethlehem, you need not discourage others any more as you are already a cursed *stambler* as are many others in this neighborhood. Your brother Henry also said that the people should not have done that to go against the government. He was scared when he came to Bethlehem and saw the people with weapons. (A line of the original here cannot be translated.) So Earl* is a devil as you and John Sheret. I say in case of an outbreak I will burn your house and barn and will shoot you and your brother dead wherever I shall detect you cursed *stamblers*. If it would not be for your brother Henry most surely Bethlehem would receive its deserving reward. The cursed advice would be frustrated. And you are never safe in your house. You and Earl* are cursed *stambles* knaves one as the other else you would not dissuade the people who are for liberty.

These are the weapons for your slaughter.

---

*Eyerley.

# The Fries Rebellion.

## CHAPTER I.

### Cause of the Rebellion; John Fries.

Between the close of the Revolution and the end of the Century, three events transpired in the United States that gave serious alarm to the friends of republican institutions.

The first of these, known in history as "Shays' Rebellion," was an unlawful combination in Massachusetts, 1786, directed against the State Government. Its head and front was Daniel Shays,[1] who had been a Captain in the Continental army, and left behind him the reputation of a brave and faithful officer The outbreak was soon quelled, but not before some of the misguided participants had paid the penalty with their lives. The second event, in the order of time, was the "Whiskey Insurrection,"[2] in the southwestern counties of Pennsylvania, 1792. It reached such magnitude, by the fall of 1794, that

---

[1] Daniel Shays, born 1747, at Hopkinton, Mass., served as ensign at the battle of Bunker's Hill, and attained the rank of Captain in the Continental Army. In 1786 he took part in the popular movement in Western Massachusetts for the redress of alleged grievances, and became the leader in the rebellion which bears his name. Shays, after being pardoned, removed to Vermont and thence to New York, where he died Sept. 29, 1825. In his old age he was allowed a pension for his services during the Revolution.

[2] The "Whiskey Insurrection" was a disturbance in the south-western section of Pennsylvania, caused by Congress imposing a tax on all ardent spirits distilled in the United States three years previously. The object of the tax was to improve the revenues of the government. It is charged that Genet, the French minister, and his partizans incited the people of the distilling regions to resist the tax collectors. The disaffected rose in arms. Washington issued two proclamations warning the insurgents to disperse but, instead of obeying, they fired upon and captured the officers of the government. A military force 15,000 strong, was then organized and sent into the disturbed district, to enforce the law, but the insurgents had already scattered when the troops arrived. The whiskey tax was a measure of the Federal party.

(1)

President Washington sent a large body of troops, under Governor Henry Lee,[3] of Virginia, into the disaffected district. The force was so imposing the insurgents abandoned their organization and returned to their homes. The third attempt was that of which we write, the "Fries Rebellion." This took place in contigious parts of Bucks'[4] and Northampton counties, in the Fall and Winter of 1798-99, and is so called from the name of the leader, John Fries, who was mainly instrumental in creating this opposition to the Federal authority. In each case the disturbance was caused in whole, or in part, by what the people considered an unjust and unlawful tax, and they resisted putting it in force. In the two latter cases the assessments to be made were of an unusual character, though not heavy in amount, and the opposition to it was caused, no doubt, by want of correct information, and not a settled design to interfere with the execution of the law. The history of the Fries Rebellion proves, quite conclusively, the outbreak was of this character, and, if proper means had been taken by the authorities to explain the law and its necessity, to the disaffected, the extreme measures taken by the general government need not have been resorted to. It was fortunate, however, the trouble was brought to a close without the loss of life or bloodshed, and the bitterness engendered was not permanent.

During the Administration of John Adams, the frequent depredations of the French upon our commerce, and their disregard of our rights on the high seas, as a neutral power to the sanguinary conflict then devastating Europe, induced the belief that war with France was unavoidable. Congress, ac-

---

[3] Governor Henry Lee, Virginia, who commanded the troops of the Government in the "Whiskey Insurrection," was the famous "Light Horse Harry" of the Revolution, and rendered Washington distinguished service as a partizan cavalry officer. He was born in Westmoreland county, Va., January 29, 1756. He was appointed by Congress to deliver the funeral oration on Washington, 1799.

[4] Bucks, one of the three original counties of Pennsylvania, and organized with Philadelphia and Chester, 1683, lies in the south-eastern coroner of the State, Northampton joining it on the northwest and Montgomery, cut off from Philadelphia, 1782, bounds Bucks on the southwest. The district, where opposition to the House tax law prevailed, was settled mainly by Germans; there was no opposition to speak of outside of a few townships in the upper end of Bucks and the lower end of Northampton. Berks was formed from Chester, Philadelphia and Lancaster, 1798.

cordingly, made preparation for such emergency should it arise. The military and naval forces of the country were increased, and General Washington, then living in retirement at Mount Vernon, was appointed to the command of the armies about to be called into the field. In view of the impending danger to the country, Congress took such other measures as the President thought requisite, some of which clothed him with almost despotic power. The act, known as the "Alien and Sedition Laws," gave him authority to send obnoxious persons out of the country, at pleasure, and to place others in arrest accused of speaking, or writing, in disrespectful terms of the government. In connection with these measures Congress made provision to carry on the war, now thought to be near at hand, by laying a direct tax to be assessed and collected by agents appointed by the Federal government.

On July 9, 1798, an act was passed providing "for the valuation of lands and dwelling houses and the enumeration of slaves within the United States." For making the valuation and enumeration, required by the act, the States were divided into districts, and, for each district, a commissioner was appointed by the President with a fixed salary. It was made the duty of the commissioners to sub-divide these districts into assessment districts, and, for each, appoint one principal and as many assistants as might be required. The assessors were to make out a list of houses, lands and slaves, and afterward to value and assess them. On July 14 Congress passed an additional act, entitled "An Act to lay and collect a direct tax within the United States," fixing the amount to be raised at $2,000,000, of which $237,177.72 was the portion allotted to Pennsylvania. The rates of assessments to be made under this act were as follows: Where the dwelling and outhouses, on a lot not exceeding two acres, were valued at more than $100 and not exceeding $500, there was to be assessed a sum equal to two-tenths of one per cent. on the valuation. As the houses and lands increased in value the rates were increased in proportion, so that a house, worth $30,000, would pay a tax equal to one per cent. of its value. By this means rich and poor alike contributed their share of the burden according to their ability to pay. Upon each slave there was assessed a tax of 50 cents. The fourth section of the act provided for the appointment of collectors, and the duties were to be discharged under instructions from the Secretary of the Treasury.

Upon the announcement of the passage of these acts of Congress, and their publication, discontent began to manifest itself. They were denounced as unconstitutional, unjust and oppressive, and the government charged with acting in a tyrannical manner. The odium already resting on Mr. Adams' Administration was increased, and new enemies made on all sides. Politicians, who seized upon it to bring the Administration into disrepute, were governed by selfish purposes, but we must credit the masses with honest motives. Following so soon, after the passage of the Alien and Sedition Laws, gave the House Tax Law greater unpopularity than it really merited, or would have received at any other time. The feeling of the country was very much aroused before its passage, and this added fuel to the flame.

The law was violently denounced in Pennsylvania as soon as its provisions were known. At first the opposition took the form of noisy declamation, and the application of harsh ephithets to the President and his Cabinet, and was mainly confined to the counties of Bucks, Montgomery, Northampton and Berks in the eastern part of the State. From passive resistance the opposition gradually assumed the shape of overt acts. In a few instances, and before any matured plan had been agreed upon, the officers were prevented by threats from making the assessments, and, in others, were hooted at and ridiculed. So odious did it make the Administration in Bucks and Northampton, that these counties positively refused to furnish their quota, under a law recently passed, for increasing the military force of the country, and not a man was furnished by them. The opposition had assumed such alarming character by the Winter and Spring of 1799 the President deemed it his duty to send a large body of troops into these counties to quell the disturbance and enforce the law. In order to give our readers an intelligent and accurate account of this outbreak, it will be necessary to take up the thread of events from the passage of the acts of Congress that led to it.

Immediately on the passage of the law, the Secretary of the Treasury took the proper steps to carry it out. The act of July 9 divided Pennsylvania into nine districts, the third being composed of the counties of Bucks and Montgomery, and the fifth of Northampton, Luzerne and Wayne, with the following named commissioners:

1st District, Israel Wheeler,   5th District, Jacob Eyerley,[6]
2d      "     Paul Zantzenger,  6th      "    Michael Schmyser,
3d      "     Seth Chapman,[5]  7th      "    Thomas Grant, Jr.,
4th     "     Collinson Reed,   8th      "    Samuel Davidson,
              9th District, Isaac Jenkinson.

Jacob Eyerley, commissioner for the fifth district, and a resident of Northampton, was commissioned sometime in the month of August and took the oath of office. Almost as soon as qualified, he was requested, by the Secretary of the Treasury, to find suitable persons to serve as assessors in his division. He had no trouble as far as the counties of Luzerne and Wayne were concerned, but, in Northampton, only two persons were named in connection with the appointment. There appeared to be a general indisposition among the people to accept office under the law.

The fourth section of the act of July 9 required the commissioners, as soon as possible after their appointment, to meet and make provision for carrying out the act. The board assembled at Reading,[7] Berks county, October 22, nearly all the members present. Each commissioner presented a plan of his division and divided it into a suitable number of assessment districts. They also furnished a list of persons qualified for assessors, which was forwarded to the Secretary of the Treasury who was authorized to reduce the

---

[5] Seth Chapman, commissioner for the Third District, and citizen of Bucks county, received his commission and instruction early in the autumn and immediately qualified. He was a relative of James Chapman and possibly a brother.

[6] Jacob Eyerley was a Moravian and a man of some influence.

[7] Reading, the county seat of Berks, was laid out in the Autumn of 1748, on a tract of 450 acres for which warrants had been taken out by John and Samuel Finney, 1733. It is now a prosperous and wealthy city of some 70,000 inhabitants.

number. A form of warrant was agreed upon and signed by the commissioners. The assessors were ordered to meet at an early day, when the commissioners would qualify and give them the necessary instructions.

Bucks county was divided into two collection districts, one composed of the twelve upper townships, for which were appointed one principal and five assistants; James Chapman,[8] Richland, being the principal, and John Rodrock,[9] Plumstead; Everhard Foulke,[10] Richland, Cephas Childs,[11] Samuel Clark, Milford, and one other assistant. Childs took the oath of office November 5, and no doubt the others were qualified about the same time. The assessors met at Rodrock's the latter part of December, after being qualified. Here the last preliminaries were arranged prior to making the attempt to carry the law into effect. Each assessor was given charge of two townships, and allowed a choice of the ones he would assess.

---

[8] James Chapman was born in Springfield township, and at this time was living in Richland, although I do not know when he moved into it. He lived on a farm some years ago the property of P. Mayer, on the road to Milford Square, one mile west of Quakertown. He belonged to Richland meeting, 1781, when he and ten other leading members were disowned for subscribing the oath of allegiance to the Colonies. The Chapman family is one of the oldest in the county, the first ancestor in America immigrating from England and settling in Wrightstown township, 1684. The Hon. Henry Chapman, lately deceased, Doylestown, was a lineal descendant of the first settler. Seth Chapman, one of the assessors, was a member of the same family. For a further account of James Chapman see chapter 9th.

[9] John Rodrock was a resident of Plumstead township when appointed, but I do not know that he was born there. He kept the tavern at what is now Plumsteadville, on the Easton pike, then known as "Rodrock's tavern," and this is where the assessors held their first meeting. He kept it down to about seventy-five years ago, and was the only house there. In 1762 it was called "James Hart's tavern." Rodrock owned about 300 acres of land in the vicinity, at his death, more than a half century ago. The village now contains 25 dwellings, with tavern, store, a brick church and extensive carriage works.

[10] Everard Foulke was a member of the Foulke family, Richland, in the neighborhood of Quakertown, and was probably appointed from that township. They were Friends. His first ancestor in this country was Edward Foulke, who came from North Wales, 1698, and settled in Gwynedd township, Montgomery county, and from there removed to Richland. The late Benjamin Foulke, Quakertown, was a descendant of the same common ancestor as Everard.

[11] Cephas Childs, or Child, the correct spelling, was of a Plumstead family, but I do not know that he lived there when appointed. A Cephas Child, or Childs, was there as early as about 1716, and was a Friend. He was a member of the Assembly, 1747-48. Among the descendants of the first settler, was the late Colonel Cephas G. Child, Philadelphia. A Cephas Child died in Plumstead in 1815, at the age of 90, probably his son, or grandson.

When it became known the assessments were actually to be made, and the tax collected under the "odious" law, the hostility of the people, which had somewhat abated since its passage, broke out anew in some localities. The excitement soon reached fever heat. The tax became the general subject of conversation throughout the country, and was discussed in the taverns, stores, at all public gatherings, and at every point where two or more persons came together. As is always the case in times of high excitement, the authors of the law were denounced in unmeasured terms, and both its object and provisions misrepresented. The most extravigant stories were put in circulation as to the intention of the government, and such a state of fear had seized upon the minds of the middle and lower classes, people were really alarmed for their personal safety. Many considered Mr. Adams a despot, and the act was viewed as the most oppressive that had ever disgraced a statute book. In this condition of things it is not in the least strange that a determination to resist the law should manifest itself. The opposition appears to have been more general in Milford[12] township, in Bucks, and in some of the border townships of Northampton county, where the inhabitants early made open demonstration to resist the assessors. In Milford the officers were wholly unable to comply with the law, and there the houses remained unassessed for some time after the assessment had been made in other parts of the district. The most active man in stirring up opposition to the Federal aushorities, and who, in fact, was the head and front of all the disturbance, was John Fries, Milford, who had the countenance and support of many of his neighbors and friends, of whom John Getman and Frederick Heany, after himself, were the boldest and most active participants in the rebellion.

It would be an easy matter, were we disposed to indulge in romance and present fictitious characters to the reader, to convert the leaders in this disturbance into heroes and clothe them with imaginary qualities; but, as we profess to deal

---

[12] Milford township, in the northwest coroner of Bucks county, was settled by Germans as early as 1725, and organized, 1734. It is one of the largest and most populous townships in the county, and is a fine agricultural region.

only with facts, and intend to write a correct account of the outbreak, 1798-99, such license is forbidden. Fries, Heany and Getman were plain, honest Germans only, and it is extending ordinary charity to suppose them to have been governed by sincere motives in the course they took.

John Fries, the leading spirit of the insurrection and came of parentage in the lower walks of life, was born in Hatfield[13] township, Montgomery county, about 1750. At 20 he was married to Margaret Brunner, daughter of David Brunner, White Marsh,[14] near Mather's Mill.[15] John was brought up to work, and, when old enough, was apprenticed to the coopering trade, which he learned. At twenty-five himself and wife, and their two children, removed to Bucks county settling in Milford township. We are not imformed as to the exact locality, but were told by his son Daniel that Joseph Galloway[16] gave him permission to build a house on his land at Boggy Creek, and occupy it as long as he wished, which offer he accepted. We have no means of knowing what length of time Fries lived there, nor when he changed his residence, but, at the time of the outbreak, we find him living in a small

---

[13] Hatfield township, Montgomery county, is bounded on the northeast by Bucks county. It was laid out about 1741 and probably derived its name from the parish and town of Hatfield, Hertfordshire, England. The population is over 2000. In 1785 it contained one tavern, two grist mills, one saw mill and one tannery. It is 3¼ miles long by 3 miles wide, with an area of 7100 acres.

[14] Whitemarsh township, Montgomery, lies in the Schuylkill Valley. It has an area of 8697 acres, and is one of the most populous townships in the county. In the quality of its limestone, marble and iron ores it is not surpassed in the State. "Whitemarsh lime," for whitewashing, finds its way all over the country. It was settled as early as 1685. It is rich in Revolutionary incidents, and, within its limits, some important movements were made by the two opposing armies in Fall of 1777 and Winter of 1777-78. It is cut by the North Pennsylvania railroad and is twelve miles from Philadelphia.

[15] Mather's mill is in Whitemarsh township, Montgomery county, near the intersection of the Bethlehem and Skippack turnpike, a mile below Fort Washington. It was built by Edward Farmer, 1705; rebuilt, 1814, by Mather, and is now or was lately owned by the Otterson estate. The mill is on the Wissahickon creek. Edward Farmer came to America with his father, 1685, and settled in Whitemarsh. He became prominent in affairs, and died November 3, 1745, in his 73d year.

[16] The Galloways came from Maryland to Philadelphia, where Joseph was born about 1730 and marrying Grace Growden, removed to Bucks county. He owned a large landed estate in Bucks that came through his wife. He abandoned the Whig cause during the Revolution, and went to England, where he died, 1803. He was active in the early part of the struggle; was a member of the first American Congress, 1774, and, at that time, no man stood higher in the Province. He was a lawyer, and a man of great ability.

log house near the Sumneytown road, two miles from Charlestown," on a lot that belonged to William Edwards, father of Caleb Edwards," deceased, Quakertown." He probably did not follow the coopering business long, if at all, after his removal into Bucks county, for the earliest information we have of him shows he was then persuing the calling of a vendue cryer, which he followed to the day of his death, and for which he seems to have been especially adapted. This occupation led him to travel all over his own, and neighboring townships, affording him an opportunity of becoming well acquainted with the country and the people. He had ten children: Solomn, John, Daniel, a second John, and a fifth which died in infancy before it had been named; Mary, Elizabeth, Sarah, Catharine and Margaret. Of these ten children Solomon and Daniel were the last to die, both aged men, who had already reached more than man's allotted years. Daniel, the younger of the two, was born at " Boggy Creek," May, 1782.

When the contest between Great Britain and her American Colonies came on, 1776, John Fries espoused the cause of his country, and became an active patriot. He was already enrolled in the militia and had command of a company. We

[17] Charlestown, now called Trumbauersville, a place of some sixty families, is built for half a mile along the road leading from Philadelphia to Allentown. At the time of the Fries Rebellion it could not have had more than one or two dwellings, besides the tavern, now known as the Eagle. It is the seat of cigar factories, and, at one time, turned out 2,000,000 a year. The first church building was erected 1769; rebuilt, 1805, and again 1868. It is now a Union church.

[18] Caleb Edwards was probably a descendant of John Edwards, who came with his wife from Abington, Montgomery county, to the neighborhood of Quakertown about 1730 with the Morrisses, Heackocks, Jamisons, Joneses and others. He must have been appointed from Richland or a neighboring township.

[19] Quakertown, Richland township, is at the intersection of the Milford Square and Newtown, Hellertown and Philadelphia roads, all opened at an early day. Here a little hamlet began to form over a century and half ago, and as the settlers were principally members of the Society of Friends, the name "Quakertown" was given it. A tavern was opened as early as 1770; a post office, 1803; a public library founded 1795; and it was incorporated into a borough in 1854. The population was 863 in 1870, and 2169 in 1890. In 1874 the borough limits were extended to include Richland Centre, a village that had grown up about the station on the North Penn. Railroad, a mile to the east. The population of the borough is about 3000. Quakertown is the centre of a rich and populous country.

are not able to say at what period he was first called into service, but we know he was on active duty 1777, for, in the Fall of that year, his company being of the militia was called out from Bucks county to re-enforce the Continental Army, and was with Washington at White Marsh and Camp Hill.[20] In the Spring of the following year he commanded a company in the action at Crooked Billet,[21] under General John Lacey,[22] and shared the dangers and defeat of the day. Nearly twenty years later, we find him in command of a company of militia, from this county, in the Whiskey Insurrection. In these military positions it is to be presumed he served his country faithfully.

---

[20] "Camp Hill" is an elevation in Whitemarsh township, Montgomery county, Pa., and so named because a portion of the Continental Army occupied it during the Fall, 1777, in the operations following the occupation of Philadelphia by the British. It lies on the left of the North Pennsylvania Railroad below Fort Washington Station, the next station below it being known as "Camp Hill," on the west side of the railroad. The contiguous country was the scene of military operations of that period by Washington's army.

[21] The "Crooked Billet," the present Hatboro, a village of a thousand inhabitants, is in Moreland township, Montgomery county, Pa., half a mile from the Bucks county line, on the North-East Pennsylvania Railroad. It has a bank, a weekly newspaper, an academy, three churches, and a valuable library, founded, 1755. It is thought to have been first settled by John Dawson, who, with his wife and daughter, and probably two sons, came from London to Pennsylvania, 1710. He was a hatter and a member of Friends' Meeting. The place was called "Crooked Billett" from a crooked stick of wood painted on the sign that hung at the tavern door in ye olden time.

[22] John Lacey, captain in the Continental Army and subsequently a Brigadier General of militia in the Revolution, was born in Buckingham township, Bucks county, Pa., 1755. The family were members of the Society of Friends, and immigrated from the Isle of Wight, England, and settled in Wrightstown among the first settlers. He was commissioned captain in the 4th Pennsylvania regiment, commanded by Col. Anthony Wayne, January 5, 1776; serving in the campaign in Canada of that year, returning home on the recruiting service in December. He shortly afterward resigned his commission, because of some unjust treatment by Colonel Wayne, but continued his activity in the cause of the Colonies. He was commissioned a Sub-Lieutenant of Bucks county, March 22, 1777; a Brigadiere General of the State, January 9, 1778, before he was 23, taking the field shortly afterward. During that Winter and Spring he had command of the country between the Delaware and Schuylkill, and rendered efficient service. The action at the Crooked Billet took place May 1, 1778. In 1779 General Lacey was chosen a member of the Executive Council of the State and, as such, served for two years. The 18th of January, 1781, he married a daughter of Colonel Thomas Reynolds, New Mills, now Pemberton, N. J., whither he removed the Fall of that year, or beginning of 1782. He entered into the iron business, and died there February 17, 1814. The late Dr. William Darlington, West Chester, Pa., married a daughter of General Lacey.

At the period of which we write, Fries was about fifty years of age. In person rather small in stature and spare, but active, hardy and well made. He was without education, except being able to read and write, with a knowledge of the rudiments of arithmetic. Nature had endowed him with good natural abilities, and he possessed a shrewd and intelligent mind. He was an easy and fluent talker, and somewhat noted for his humour and cunning; was possessed of good hard sense, and, had his mind been properly cultivated, would doubtless have been a man of mark. Personally he was brave and resolute, and unknown to fear. He is said to have possessed a species of rude eloquence which was very engaging, and gave him great control over the multitude. He was a sworn enemy to all kinds of oppression, fancied or real, and was esteemed a quiet and inoffensive man until this outbreak aroused the latent fires within him, made him notorious and his name a terror to the Administration of Mr. Adams. He had brown hair, quick and steady black eyes, of which an old neighbor, and one who formerly knew him well, told us "were as keen as the eyes of a rabbit." He had a pleasant disposition, was well liked by all, and, with many, quite a favorite. His character for honesty was above suspicion, and he was considered a sober man, though occassionally indulged in strong drink. These personal and other qualities gave him, to a considerable degree, the confidence of the community in which he lived, and enabled him to exercise a controlling influence over his neighbors and friends.

In following his occupation of vendue cryer he generally traversed the county on horseback, and, in all his wanderings, was accompanied by a small black dog named "Whiskey," to which he was greatly attached. When he entered a house it was his habit to call for "Whiskey," when the faithful little animal would come and take a seat by his side and remain until his master got up to go away. Master and dog were inseparable companions, and aged persons who knew Fries stated to us that his approach was often heralded some time before he came in sight by the appearance of "Whiskey" trotting along in advance. The favorite little dog, as will be seen, before we conclude, was the means of the betrayal of his master into the hands of his enemies.

Next to John Fries, Frederick Heaney and John Getman were the most active instigators of the disturbance. They were both residents of Milford township at the time, the former living two miles from Charlestown, the latter within half a mile of Fries' house; they were tailors by trade, and in an humble condition in life. Of their history we have been able to learn but little. Heaney was born at what is now "Stover's Mill,"[23] Rockhill township, but we do not know at what period he changed his residence to Milford. At one time he kept the tavern at Hagersville,[24] of which Christian Hager was landlord forty years ago, but we have not been able to learn the date of his residence at this place. After his pardon by Mr. Adams, Heaney returned to his home, Milford township, whence he removed to Plainfield,[25] Northampton county, where he died.[26] He gained there not only a respectable, but a somewhat influential standing in the community. He was appointed justice of the peace, and also commanded a volunteer company, which his grandson, George Heaney, commanded, 1860. After his death, which did not take place until he

---

[23] Stover's Mill is in Rockhill township, Bucks county, a few miles from Sellersville, on the North Pennsylvania Railroad, and was owned by a member of the family of that name a few years ago.

[24] Hagersville is situated on the Old Bethlehem Road, in the north-west corner of Rockhill township. It has a store, tavern, the usual village mechanics, and some dozen dwellings. At this point the road is the dividing line between Bedminster and Rockhill townships. The village took its name from Colonel George Hager, a prominent man and politician over half a century ago. He was a candidate for sheriff 1836.

[25] Plainfield township, Northampton county, was settled as early as 1730 and organized shortly after 1752, but the records of its organization are lost. It was a frontier township of Bucks county at the time of its organization.

[26] We were told by a descendant of Frederick Heaney that he was of German descent, as his name implies, his father, Johannes Horning, having immigrated from the Palatinate about 1742, and settled at what was afterward known as "Heaney's Mill," Rockhill township, Bucks county. Frederick was born there August 18, 1769. At the beginning of the present century he removed to Northampton county, where he died, 1818. Governor Simon Snyder commissioned him justice of the peace, for a district of Northampton, composed of the townships of Upper and Lower Mount Bethel and Plainfield, July 27, 1809, which office he held until his death. He was buried at Plainfield Church, near the Wind Gap. A number of his descendants live in Monroe and Northampton counties.

THE NEW YORK
PUBLIC LIBRARY

ASTOR, LENOX AND
TILDEN FOUNDATIONS.

FACSIMILE OF A THREATENING NOTICE ISSUED DURING THE FREAS' REBELLION.
ORIGINAL IN THE COLLECTION OF JOHN W. JORDAN, PHILADELPHIA.

wie ich euch vor mich auch verpflichten
ßmeblten wan ich auch vor dein brüder
frewich wer gewest so hat betsheram, nu
ewer kinder son geigt das freyßlusters
vakemrest wer freytrut worden
ind ihr seil nimer süher in eurem haus
ist ind Der nivola ist an frestüster
ßmebel gwest wir der ander sonst
indem ir den seil auch ab eram
die sei dir soresseil sint

Das ist gewer vor euch
zu schasten

had reached a green old age, his widow was twice married, and died in Plainfield, 1855, at the age of eighty-nine years. He had three sons, Charles, Samuel and Enoch, and one daughter, Elizabeth. It is related by his descendants that while the troops were in pursuit of him, a party of soldiers came to his house one night, when his wife was alone, except her little daughter, Elizabeth. They heard of threats against his life, and, hearing them coming, she jumped out of bed and put a spike over the door to prevent them getting in, and, leaving her child in the house, ran out the back door and across the fields to alarm a neighbor. When she returned with help the soldiers were gone. This child was Mrs. Edmonds, living, 1860, in Bushkill township, Northampton county, whose son, Jacob B. Edmonds, resided at Quakertown.

Getman is supposed to have been born in Rockhill township, also, but we have not been able to learn anything of his history. His brother George died near Sellersville, Bucks county, March 4, 1855, at the advanced age of 92 years, 2 months and 10 days, respected by all his friends and neighbors. He, likewise, was arrested during the trouble; was tried and convicted but received a much lighter sentence than his brother John, being fined one hundred dollars and sentenced to undergo an imprisonment of 6 months. Heaney was the owner of a small house and lot. These two men were the advisors and confederates of John Fries, Getman being the most in his confidence. They lacked the intelligence and shrewdness of their leader, but were active in the cause and rendered him important service. Such were the three men who were the head and front of the " Fries Rebellion." Thus we have related the cause of the rebellion, with some account of the principal actors in it, and, in the next chapter, we shall give our readers a brief history of the overt acts of the insurgents.

# The Fries Rebellion.

## CHAPTER II.

### The Insurgents Prepare to Resist the Law.

John Fries was probably the first to array himself against the law, immediately upon its passage and promulgation. His own intense hostility begat the desire that his neighbors and friends should agree with him in feeling, and he labored with great zeal to this end. When going about the county crying vendues, he was careful to sound the people as to how they stood upon the subject of the new tax, and was never backward in expressing his own opinion. From a warm supporter of Mr. Adams and his Administration, he suddenly became their most bitter enemy, giving vent to his feelings in terms of unmeasured denunciation. He reasoned with, persuaded, and threatened all and seemed to make it his business to create enemies to the act. He was thus active during the Fall months of 1798, and, by the end of the year, had raised a fierce opposition to the law and those who were to carry it into execution. He was particularly hostile to the house-tax, and declared openly that no assessments should be made in Milford township, nor tax collected if he could prevent it. We were informed by his son Daniel, then about eighteen, and had a distinct recollection of the events transpiring, that several private meetings were held at his father's house before any public demonstration was made. His friends and neighbors met there to talk about the law, and determine, in a quiet manner, what was best to be done. At these conferences Fries always took the lead, and his stronger mind assisted to mould the opinion of others.

The time had now arrived when some more active measures must be taken, and opinion changed to deeds. The period approached when the assessors were to commence their duties, and some public demonstration was necessary to prevent them carrying the law into effect. With this object in view, about the first of February, 1799, notices, without any names signed to them, were put up at various places in the township, calling a public meeting for Friday, the eighth, at the public house of John Klein, on the road leading to Gary's tavern, two miles southwest from Charlestown. On the day appointed, a number of persons assembled at the place of meeting late in the afternoon. The two most active and noisy men present were John Fries and George Mitchel,[1] who then kept the public house more recently occupied by Eli L. Zeigler, at the west end of Charlestown. This tavern was one of the places where the mal contents of the neighborhood assembled at evenings to talk over their grievances. Few, if any, at the meeting appear to have had a very definite idea of what should be done; they disliked the house-tax and were opposed to paying it themselves, or permitting others to do so; but, beyond this, there was no plan of opposition, at this time. The law was discussed and its authors denounced in violent terms.

Some expressed a doubt whether the bill had yet become a law. The newspapers of the day mentioned that an amendment had lately passed Congress, which seemed to confuse the understanding of the people, and rendered them undecided as to whether the law was actually in force. After the matter had been sufficiently considered and the sense of the meeting fully explained, Fries, with the assistance of the publican, Mitchel, drew up a paper that was approved and signed by about fifty of those present. What the exact import of this paper was has never been determined, as neither the original nor a copy fell into the hands of the authorities. It is supposed, however, to have contained merely a statement of the views of the signers upon the subject of the tax, and their determination to oppose the execution of the law. Before ad-

---

[1] We are not able to learn anything further of George Mitchell than is mentioned here.

journing, however, a resolution was passed requesting the assessors not to come into the township to make the assessment, until the people were better informed whether the law was really in force; and one Captain Kuyder appointed to serve a copy of the resolution upon them. Having transacted the business which brought them together, the people quietly dispersed and returned to their homes. The meeting was conducted in the most orderly and peaceable manner, and there was no appearance of disturbance on the part of anyone.

Our readers will bear in mind, that Mr. Chapman, commissioner for the counties of Bucks and Montgomery, met the assessors of the former county at the public house of Mr. Rodrock, the latter end of December, to deliver to them their instructions how to proceed in the assessments. Immediately after this meeting, these officers commenced the assessment in the respective townships assigned them. They proceeded without any trouble, or appearance of opposition, in all the townships but Milford, and even there the people, notwithstanding the late agitation and excitement against the law, quietly acquiesce in its execution. It is true they did not like it, and would rather have avoided paying the tax, but they had abandoned all intention of resisting the law. Childs and Clark had both been appointed for Milford, and, before separating, fixed upon a day when they would begin in that township. Childs had also one or two other townships assigned him, and, it was arranged between them, they should assist each other, two days at a time, alternately. As Childs had already made some assessments in his own district, he agreed to help Clark whenever he should be ready to begin the work. Before the meeting adjourned at Rodrock's, the principal assessor named an early day to meet again, and make return of what they had done. Mr. Childs went to assist Clark according to agreement, but, when he reached his house, finding the latter was not able to go on with the assessments, he returned to finish up his own district. In Milford the excitement was still running high; and as threats of serious injury had been made against the assessors, who were forbidden to enter the township, they declined to attempt it.

Fries and his friends had inflamed the minds of the people to such degree, that in some parts of the township they were almost in a condition to take up arms. The assessors met at Rodrock's, to make returns, on February 6, but as they did not complete their business that day they adjourned to meet on the 16th.

In the unsettled condition of things in Milford, the principal assessor, James Chapman, determined to take some steps to satisfy the people of that township in relation to the tax. For this purpose he thought it advisable to have a public meeting called at some convenient place, where he would explain the law, but not trusting altogether to his own judgment in the matter, he went to George Mitchel's on Monday, February 11, and consulted him. The latter agreeing with the principal assessor, he was requested to lend his assistance in getting up the meeting and assented. Word was sent to Jacob Hoover,[2] who owned and lived at a mill on Swamp creek, on the road leading from Trumbauersville to Spinnerstown, about one mile west of the former place, and the same later occupied by Jonas Graber,[3] to give notice of the meeting to the people of his neighborhood; and also to inform them they would be permitted to select their own assessor, and that any capable man whom they might name would be qualified. The offer, however, did not meet with much favor in that section of the township, and the people declined to have anything to do with it. There seemed to be a general disposition, among the friends of Mr. Adams in the township, to have a public meeting called notwithstanding the failure of the first attempt—to endeavor to reconcile matters; and Israel Roberts and Samuel Clark both saw Mitchell upon the subject. A few days after, Mr. Chapman again sent word to Mitchell to advertise a meeting, which he accordingly did, and

---

[2] The Hoovers, or Hubers, immigrated from Switzerland between 1750 and 1760, and settled in Milford township. The father's name we do not know, but his wife's was Ann, who was born 1722, died 1775, and was buried at the Trumbauersville church. Henry, one of the sons, made powder for the Penna. Committee of Safety, 1776, at a mill on Swamp creek. Another son, John Jacob, was probably the "Jacob Hoover" mentioned here.

[3] This was in 1859; the present owner we do not know.

the time fixed was the latter end of February, the place, his own tavern. The notice given was pretty general, and a large assemblage was expected.

The Jacob Hoover here spoken of was the uncle of Reuben L. Wyker, who lived near Rufe's store in Tinicum, and was active in assisting Fries. It is said he manufactured cartouch boxes for the use of the insurgents, and otherwise made himself useful to them. He escaped capture by having timely warning of the approach of the troops. George Wyker, also of Tinicum, and uncle of Reuben L., was in Philadelphia at market, at the time, and there learned that Jacob Hoover was to be arrested, and that a warrant had already been issued. Being anxious to prevent him falling into the hands of the federal authorities, he hastened home, as soon as he had sold out his marketing, to give warning of the danger. He told his father what he had heard in the city. The latter was Nicholas Wyker, who lived on the same farm where Alfred Sacket lived in more recent years, on the hillside near Rufe's store. He immediately set off for Hoover's, whom he found at home, apparently very much unconcerned, but entirely ignorant of the danger that threatened him. Even when told of the arrangements made to arrest him, he did not seem to give it much importance; but, while they were in conversation Hoover looked out the window and saw the troops coming up the road. This reminded him of the necessity of fleeing. He immediately ran out the back door, and, keeping the house between him and them, made his way to a neighboring thicket, into which he escaped. When the soldiers arrived at the house, they surrounded it and entered, but the bird had flown, and Hoover was nowhere to be found. After a thorough search, the officer gave up the pursuit and returned with his soldiers, much chagrined. Hoover kept out of harm's way until the affair had blown over, when he returned home. He afterward removed to Lewistown, in this State, where he died.

In the meantime the adjourned meeting to be holden at Rodrock's tavern, on February 16, at which the returns of the assessments were to be made, came off. All the assessors, except Mr. Clark, were there and reported the assessments had been nearly completed in all the townships except Milford, where nothing had as yet been done. The assessor of this township had been so much intimidated and threatened he was afraid to go about in the discharge of his duties. Mr. Foulke also expressed some fears of going into the township, as threats had likewise been made against him, and he anticipated trouble. This state of things changed his mind in regard to permitting the people of the township to select their own assessor, and he now gave his consent to it, hoping it would conciliate them. He used his influence with the commissioner to induce him to agree to the same, and he finally yielded and gave his permission. He notified the assessors, at the same time, that in case the people did not accept the terms offered them, and choose some person to discharge the duty, they would have to go into the township, and assist Clark to make the assessments. Proposals were made to the various assessors as to which would assume the duty, but each one had some excuse to give why he could not go, showing great unwillingness to place themselves in the way of danger. The unsettled condition of Milford alarmed them, John Fries and his friends being the terror of these officers.

The time for the meeting advertised to take place at Mitchell's had now arrived, which was holden on a Saturday, and a great many persons were at it. Everhard Foulke and James Chapman were present on the part of the assessors. The meeting was called for the purpose of reading and explaining the law, as they were extremely ignorant of its provisions and operations; but they behaved in such a disorderly manner nothing could be done. A general fear appears to have seized upon those present. Mr. Foulke used his best endeavors to remove it, but without avail. In their present state of mind, as he well knew, any explanation of the law on his part would have but little, if any, effect, and he did not even attempt it. Among the well disposed citizens present was Jacob Klein, who, at the request of Mitchell, made an effort to calm the fears of the people, but he met with no success, for the clamor and noise were so incessant he could not be heard.

Israel Roberts proposed to read the law to them, but they would not listen to him, and drowned his voice in their shouts. Conrad Marks, who afterward became an active participant in the disturbance, was at the meeting, but it does not appear that John Fries was there, which is hardly reconcileable, with his known activity in opposing the law. The assessors seeing nothing could be done toward satisfying their minds on the subject of the tax, and removing their prejudice and opposition to the law's execution, declined to take further part in the meeting and returned home.

The officers, upon this occasion, met with a signal failure in their attempt to induce the people to acquiesce in the assessments, and the result of the meeting gave encouragement to the opposition. In the subsequent trial of John Fries before the United States Court, Mr. Chapman, who was a witness on the part of the Government, gives the following account of what took place at this meeting, so far as it fell under his own observations. He says:

"I got there between one and two o'clock. Just as I got to the house, before I went in, I saw ten or twelve people coming from towards Hoover's mill; about the half of them were armed, and the others with sticks. I went into the house and twenty or thirty were there. I sat talking with some of my acquaintance that were well disposed to the laws. Conrad Marks talked a great deal in German; how oppressive it was, and much in opposition to it, seeming to be much enraged. His son, and those who came with him, seemed to be very noisy and rude; they talked in German, which as I did not know sufficiently, I paid but little attention to them. They were making a great noise; huzzaing for liberty and Democracy, damning the Tories, and the like. I let them go on, as I saw no disposition in the people to do anything toward forwarding the business. Between four and five I got up to go out; as I passed through the crowd towards the bar, they pushed one another against me.

"No offer was made to explain the law to them while I staid; they did not seem disposed to hear it.

".They did not mention my name the whole time of my being there, but they abused Eyerly and Balliett and said they had cheated the public, and what villains they were. I understood it was respecting collecting the revenue, but I did not understand near all they said. I recollect Conrad Marks said that Congress had no right to make such a law, and that he never would submit to have his house taxed.

"They seemed to think that the collectors were all such fellows; the insinuation was that they cheated the public, and made them pay, but never paid into the Treasury. After getting through the crowd to the bar, I suppose I was fifteen minutes in conversation with Mitchell; he said perhaps they were wrong, but the people were very much exasperated. Nothing very material happened, and I asked Mr. Foulke if it were not time to be going. So I got into my sleigh and went off; soon after they set up a dreadful huzza and shout."

Israel Roberts and other witnesses, on the part of the prosecution at the trial of Fries, and who was present at the meeting at Mitchel's, testified as follows:

"At the last meeting at Mitchell's there appeared a disposition to wait till they should have assistance from some other place. It was said that a letter had arrived to George Mitchell, from Virginia, stating there were a number of men, I think ten thousand, on their way to join them; the letter was traced from one to another, through six or eight persons, till at last it came from one who was not there. Some of the company at that time were armed and in uniform. I do not recollect what was said when the letter was mentioned, but they appeared to be more opposed to the law than they were before.

"At the meeting at George Mitchel's, at which Mr. Foulke and Mr. Chapman were present, which was held for the purpose of explaining the law, there were a number, about twelve came up in uniform, and carrying a flag with "Liberty" on it. They came into the house and appeared to be very much opposed to the law, and in a very bad humour. I proposed to read the law to them; and they asked me how I came to advertise the meeting ; I told them I did it with the consent of a few others; one of them asked me what business I had to do it ; I told him we did it to explain the law. He looked me in the face and said, 'We don't want any of your damned laws, we have laws of our own,' and he shook the muzzle of his musket in my face, saying, 'This is our law and we will let you know it.' There were four or five who wished to hear it, but others forbid it, and said it should not be read, and it was not done."

On his way home from the meeting, Mr. Chapman stopped at the public house of Jacob Fries, who then kept the tavern more recently occupied by George L. Pheister, at the east end of Trumbauersville, where he waited for Mr. Foulke to come up, who arrived soon after. Clark was also there. Mr. Chapman had a conversation with him upon the subject of taking the rates in the township, when he declined to have anything more to do with it. He gave as a reason for this course that it would not be safe for him to undertake the assessments, and that he did not feel justified in endangering his life in order to assist to have the law carried into execution. He thus washed his hands of the whole business, and resigned his commission. It was now evident to Chapman and Foulke, that the other assessors would be obliged to make the assessments in Milford, if they were made at all, and they deemed it their duty to take immediate steps to have it done. They agreed to meet the assessors at Quakertown, on March 4, in order to commence the work, and, before they left for home, Mr. Chapman asked each one to be present at the time and place appointed. When the day arrived for the meeting, but three of the assessors attended, Rodrock, Childs and Foulke, in addition to the principal, Mr. Chapman. They waited until evening without transacting any business, expecting others would arrive but none came, when they adjourned to meet at the house of Mr. Chapman, at nine o'clock the next morning.

As soon as it became noised about that the assessors had resolved to come into the township to take the rates, those opposed to the law renewed their activity against it. The people were told by the leaders that the assessments must not be made, and force would be used to prevent it, if necessary. The information that the assessors, who were now looked upon as enemies to republican institutions were coming, increased the excitement, and the people began active measures to oppose them. Captain Kuyder, who was in command of a company of militia, called them into service to assist in driving the assessors out of the township. He notified his men to meet him at his mill, on March 6, where some fifteen or twenty assembled. Early in the morning, while he was abroad in the neighborhood, he met his acquaintance, William Thomas, whom he invited to go to the mill and see his men. He accepted the invitation and accompanied the Captain there. His men were getting together. When he arrived he found a number already assembled, a portion of them armed and others soon came up. After remaining a little while the Captain ordered his men to take up the march for the tavern of Jacob Fries, Trumbauersville.

By the time they reached the village a considerable number of stragglers had been attracted, who helped to swell the throng. They marched along the main road until they came to the tavern, when they drew up in front of it and halted. Here a number more joined them, making about thirty in all. The people assembled expressed a desire to see the assessors, whom they knew were somewhere in the township making assessments; and a couple of horsemen were sent off to hunt them up and notify them they were wanted. They were instructed, in case they should find them, to take them prisoners, and either conduct them to Quakertown or bring them to Fries' tavern. Soon after the messengers had left, it was proposed that Captain Kuyder's company and the rest of the people assembled, should march to Quakertown and they immediately started down the road for that place. They presented a somewhat martial, but very irregular, appearance; the greater part being either armed with guns or clubs and accompanied with drum and fife. As they passsed through the country they attracted much attention, and the sounds of their martial music were heard " far o'er hill and dale." They, who were not cognizant of the movement, and hardly knew what to make of the demonstration, went to the roadside to see what was going on. As they marched along the road they increased in number, and, by the time they reached their destination, there were more than a hundred in the company. This movement was the commencement of the overt acts of resistance, and had an important bearing on the subsequent conduct of those who became insurgents in name and deed.

# The Fries Rebellion.

## CHAPTER III.

### Fries Captures the Assessors.

The three assessors, Chapman, Foulke and Childs, met, on the morning of March 5, at the house of Mr. Chapman as had been agreed upon, and thence proceeded into Milford township to make the assessments. They thought it advisable to to call upon Clark, in the first instance, and see if they could not prevail upon him to go with them and divide the township, so as to complete their work in a short time. When they arrived at his house he was absent from home, and it was thought best for Mr. Chapman to go in search of him. Learning he had gone to assist one of his neighbors to move, he went to Jacob Fries" tavern to wait for him to return. In a little while he came. Upon being asked to assist in assessing the township he positively refused, saying he might as well pay his fine, even if it should take all the property he had. Finding that nothing could be done with him, the subject was dropped. While Mr. Chapman was at the tavern, John Fries came up. After passing the compliments of the day, Fries remarked to him he understood he had been insulted at one of the meetings in the township, which, he said, would not have been the case had he been present, and expressed his regret at the rudeness with which the assessor had been treated. The following interview then took place between the two, as sworn to on the trial of Fries :

"I told him (Fries) I thought they were very wrong in opposing the law as they did; he signified that he thought they were not, and that the rates should not be taken by the as-

---

[1] Jacob Fries' tavern, torn down many years ago, was situated in the rocky part of Milford township, in a valley, about a mile below Milford Centre, and two hundred yards from a public road. The road passed by the house in early times, but was changed. The house was a long, story and a half, stone and log building. It was not a tavern for more than half a century before it was torn down. The property was once owned by John Keiper.

sessors. I told him the rates would certainly be taken, and that the assessors were then in the township taking them. I repeated it to him, and he answered, 'My God! if I were only to send that man (pointing to one standing by,) to my house to let them know they were taking the rates, there would be five or seven hundred men under arms here to-morrow morning by sunrise.' He told me he would not submit to the law. I told him I thought the people had more sense than to rise in arms to oppose the law in that manner; if they did, government must certainly take notice of it, and send an armed force to enforce the law. His answer was, 'if they do, we will soon try who is the strongest.' I told him they certainly would find themselves mistaken respecting their force; he signified he thought not; he mentioned to me the troop of horse in Montgomery county, and the people at Upper and Lower Milford,[2] and something about infantry who were ready to join. He said he was very sorry for the occasion, for, if they were to rise, God knew where it would end; the consequences would be dreadful; I told him they would be obliged to comply; he then said huzza, it *shall* be as it is in France, or *will* be as it is in France, or something to that effect. He then left me and and went off."

While Mr. Chapman was waiting for Clark at Jacob Fries' tavern, and holding the strange interview with John Fries, the other assessors were engaged in taking the rates around the township. The first house they came to was Daniel Weidner's, at the west end of Trumbauersville, and occupied by Geo. Zeigler, 1859. Childs went in first and told Mr. W. that he had come in order to take the assessment under the revenue law of the United States. He appeared to be in a bad humour at the proceeding, and declined to give any information of his property. The assessor reasoned with him, and pointed out the impropriety of his conduct and what would be the consequence of his opposing the law. He was told he might have ten days to consider the matter, at the end of which time he would be able to determine what he ought to do. He professed not to know whether the law was in force, and said many other things in extenuation of his conduct;

---

[2] Upper and Lower Milford townships in Lehigh county, originally Upper Milford, in Bucks, fell into Northampton when that county was cut off from Bucks, 1752, and into Lehigh when that county was organized, 1812. At what time Upper Milford was divided we do not know.

charged the assessor with receiving very high wages, &c. Mr. Childs explained that the law was in force and how a committee of Congress had reported against the expediency of repealing it. At last, Weidner, overcome by persuasion, or argument, consented to be assessed and gave up his property, saying to the assessor, "take it now, since it must be done." Childs then continued on his round, walking and leading his horse from house to house, until he reached Mitchel's tavern,³ where he found the other two assessors, who had arrived a little while before. Weidner got there in advance and was again railing out against the law; and said that the houses of high value were to pay nothing, while smaller ones, and of small value, were to pay high. He was again reasoned with, and finally became apparently reconciled, and gave up an additional piece of property to be assessed. He seemed to take the matter much at heart, however, and exclaimed, "They will ruin me; what shall I do?" The assessors then continued on their way toward Jacob Fries' tavern, where they were to meet the principal assessors by appointment, assessing several houses as they went along. They had assessed some fifty or sixty houses in the whole, up to this point, and had done it without opposition. In every case but one the people were at home, and there a notice was left. They arrived at the tavern a little before dinner. As Mr. Childs was going into the door he was met by John Fries, who shook him by the hand, said he was glad to see him, and asked him to take a drink.

The assessors dined at Jacob Fries'. After dinner, and while they were sitting at the fire, John Fries came into the room. He addressed himself to Mr. Foulke and Mr. Chapman, and said they were men he greatly esteemed, and was sorry they had placed themselves in that position. He here proclaimed his opposition to the law; and said "I now warn you not to go to another house to take the rates; if you do you will be hurt." Without waiting for a reply he turned upon his heel and went out of the room. He seemed irritated and in anger. He said nothing more to them while they remained there. After a conference, the assessors concluded to

---

³ I have not been able to locate Mitchel's tavern, further than to say it was in Milford township.

pay no attention to the threat of John Fries, but proceed with the assessments. While at the tavern, Mr. Childs took the rates of Jacob Fries' house to which no opposition was made. It was then agreed that Rodrock and Foulke should go together, and Childs by himself to assess the houses of some who were known to be quiet and orderly people. They then mounted their horses and rode away in discharge of their duty. They found a marked difference, between the English and German, to be assessed; with the former they had no difficulty, except at one place, where the family said there were some bad people living in the neighborhood who would do them injury if they submitted to the rates. Messrs. Rodrock and Foulke continued on until about sunset without meeting any hindrance, or seeing any sign of opposition to the execution of the law. They were now going to the house of a man named Singmaster, and, as they turned down a lane out of the public road, they heard some person halloo to them; when, stopping and looking round, they saw John Fries and five men coming toward them. Fries was in front, and upon coming up he said he had warned them not to proceed with the assessments, but as they would not obey him he had now come to take them prisoners. Rodrock asked him by what authority he had stopped them, to which he made no reply, but immediately grappled for the bridle of his horse. He wheeled the horse around at the moment, which caused Fries to miss the bridle and catch the rider by the coat tail, but the latter succeeded in tearing away and freeing himself from his grasp. Fries then rode off, but, before he had gone far, he turned about and approached the assessor again. He now cursed Rodrock, and, remarked to him, if he had a horse he would catch him. He offered no further insult, but returned to his companions. Mr. Foulke was less fortunate. The comrades of Fries surrounded him and secured him without resistance; but when in their power they offered him no injury, but treated him with kindness. When Fries returned to his men and found Mr. Foulke in their hands, he at once directed them to let him go, giving as a reason that as they were not able to catch Mr. Rodrock, they would not detain him. As the assessor was released Fries remarked to him, "I will have seven hundred men together to-morrow, and I will come to your house, and let you know we are opposed to the law." Being at liberty once more the assessors proceeded to the house of Philip Singmaster, who lived on the road leading from Trumbauersville to Philadelphia, half a mile from the former place, and in a house occupied by Zeno Frantz, 1859. They found him at home, and, upon informing him of their business, were permitted to assess his house without opposition. While here Mr. Childs rejoined them as had been agreed upon when they parted company at the tavern of Jacob Fries. They now compared opinions, and came to the unanimous conclusion they would not be justified in further attempt to take the rates in Milford township, on account of the violent opposition of the inhabitants, led on by John Fries; and the principal assessor was to give notice of this determination to the commissioners. They thereupon ceased to make assessments in the township and turned their faces homeward on the afternoon of March 6.

Meanwhile the insurgents continued their march toward Quakertown, where they arrived about noon, or shortly after. In a little while the party of Capt. Kuyder was joined by John Fries and companions and several others. They halted at the tavern of Enoch Roberts, the same kept by Peter Smith, 1859, when those on horseback dismounted, and, as many as could, went into the house. The scene around the tavern was one of noise and confusion, while those inside were no less boisterous. They were hallooing, and cursing and swearing; the most violent were denouncing John Adams, the house-tax, and the officers who were to execute the law; some were drumming and fifing, apparently endeavoring to drown the hum of confused voices in the strains of martial music, and numerous other ways were resorted to, to give vent to their feelings. The bar of Mr. Roberts was pretty generously patronized, and that liquor flowed so freely the excitement and confusion were increased. Fries, expecting the assessors to come that way on their return home, he had made up his mind to arrest them if nothing transpired to interfere with his arrangements.

When the assessors ended their conference at Philip Singmaster's, after having assessed him, they started directly homeward, having to pass through Quakertown their most direct road. Messrs. Foulke and Rodrock rode together, while Mr. Childs preceded them a short distance. When they arrived at the village, they found it in possession of the crowd of people already mentioned, under the control of John Fries and Conrad Marks. Some were in uniform and others in their usual working clothes; some were armed with guns, and others carried clubs. The noise and confusion they made were heard some time before the assessors reached the town. The testimony, given on the trial, shows they were congregated at two public houses, one already mentioned as being kept by Enoch Roberts, whereas the other was called "Zeller's tavern." We have been at considerable trouble to locate this latter public house, but have been unable to do so. The house, in which Richard Green lived, 1859, on the road to the railroad station, is said to stand on the site of an old tavern which may have been the one the witnesses called "Zeller's." On the other hand it is said, by the old residents of Quakertown, that Enoch Roberts had a son-in-law named N. B. Sellers, who assisted him to keep the public house he then occupied. The name of Zeller may have been intended for Sellers, and is possibly a misprint in the report of the trial, both meaning one and the same place.

When the insurgents saw the assessors coming they set up a great shout, and, as soon as they had approached within hailing distance, ordered them to stop. This they did not heed, as they had determined not to place themselves in their power if it could be avoided. As they entered the village Messrs. Foulke and Rodrock separated, and did not ride in together, Mr. Childs having already stopped at the house of a neighbor just on the edge of the town. Rodrock now rode in advance, and, when he had passed about half through the crowd, without giving heed to their commands to stop, they started to run after him from both sides of the road, some carrying clubs and others muskets, and made motions as if they intended to strike him. John Fries was standing upon the porch of the tavern, and when he saw Rodrock coming up he called out to him to stop, but, paying no attention to it, some of the men ran after him. The assessor, seeing himself pursued, wheeled his horse and demanded of Fries what he wanted with him. This seemed to excite the men the more, and they replied to him with curses, and ordered him, in an authoritative tone, to deliver himself up. To this he replied he would not do it while they addressed him in such language as they had applied to him. Some one in the crowd then gave the order to fire at him, when two men standing near the tavern door pointed their guns but did not fire. He now rode off toward home, and when they saw him making his escape, they again commanded him to stop; some making demonstrations to get their horses and pursue him, but they did not. When he reached the house of Daniel Penrose, seeing Jacob Fries and John Jamieson there, he halted and related to them what had taken place. He appeared to be much alarmed; said that Foulke and Childs had been captured, and was afraid they would be killed. He requested Jamieson to return to the village, and prevent them being hurt, which he declined doing unless Rodrock would accompany him; but he was finally prevailed upon to go. He found the two assessors in the hands of the mob but not injured.

The other two assessors were less fortunate both falling into the hands of the enemy. As Mr. Foulke, who was some little ways in the rear of Mr. Rodock, approached Roberts' tavern, the crowd ran out to surround him. Some took hold of the horse's bridle, while others, among them Captain Kuyder, seized his person. John Fries came up at this moment and commanded him to dismount, saying that he desired to speak to him, while the surrounding crowd demanded he should be pulled off his horse. There was great danger of violent hands being laid on him, and he began to be alarmed at his situation. At this critical moment, the two Hoovers, John and Jacob, came to his assistance, and interfered with the excited multitude in his behalf. They ordered the mob to desist from their insults, and let Mr. Foulke alone, who would get off his horse without any compulsion. They gave the insurgents to understand the assessors would not be injured while they could protect them. Their resolute conduct somewhat silenced the crowd. Mr. Foulke deemed it the best policy to comply with their demands, inasmuch as he was not in a condition to help himself, and therefore rode up to the tavern shed, where he dismounted, tied his horse, and went into the house. The crowd followed him and soon the bar-room was filled. Now Fries reminded him that he had warned him the day before not to assess the houses in Milford township, and yet they had done so contrary to his orders. He then demanded Foulke's papers, which were delivered to Fries, who, after reading, carefully returned, them. The assessor was now suffered to depart, Fries escorting him through the people to his horse, and holding the bridle while he mounted, when he rode off. Fries admitted to Foulke that he had violated the law, probably enough to endanger his life, and told him that he might "return him to the Court if he wanted to do so."

It will be remembered that Mr. Childs did not accompany Rodrock and Foulke into Quakertown, but stopped at the edge of it—at the house of Esquire Griffith, who lived where Joseph R. Lancaster resided, 1859, where he dismounted and went in. As he was getting off his horse, Mrs. Griffith came out of the house and told him the people had come to make him and the others prisoners, and there was a large crowd in the village waiting to catch them. A few moments after he entered the house, a little girl came into the room and said the insurgents were taking Mr. Foulke, and, upon going to the window, saw them all around him. When he saw the danger which menaced his companions, he was going out to assist them, but the family persuaded him to remain where he was, and not place himself in unnecessary danger. In a little while John Fries came to the house and saluted Childs in a friendly manner, but told him he must accompany him to where his men were; and, as he had not the power to resist, concluded he might as well yield with as good grace as possible, and thereupon consented to go. As they walked along, Fries said to Childs he had told him yesterday not to go to another house, and now they had come to make him prisoner if they found he intended to go on with the assessments. Childs replied that he and the others were obliged to fulfil their office, unless interrupted by force. When they entered the tavern, Fries addressed himself to his men and Childs, saying: " Here are my men—here is one of them." Going into the bar-room he seated himself upon a table and soon there were several around him  One man damned him and said he should go to the liberty pole and dance around it. During this time they were crowding upon him and pushing, and he received several thumps with the knees and fists. At first he was taken for Rodrock, but when it was discovered he was not, they cursed him anew for being somebody else. He then made himself known as Cephus Childs, when some one remarked he was no better than the others. They asked him a multitude of questions about the assessments; how the people liked it where he had been, whether he had taken the oath of allegiance to the United States, &c., &c. That the reader may judge of the temper the people were in, we make the following extract from the testimony of Mr. Childs, given on the trial:

"They damned the house tax and the stamp act, and called me a 'stampler,' repeatedly; they damned the Alien and Sedition laws, and finally all the laws; the government and all the laws the present government had made. They damned the Constitution, also. They did not mention what constitution, whether of this State or of the United States. They damned the Congress, and damned the President, and all the friends to government, because they were all tories, as none were friends to the present government but the tories. They said they would not have the government, nor the President, and they would not live under such a damned government ; 'we will have Washington;' others said no, ' No, we will have Jefferson, he is a better man than Adams; huzzah for Jefferson.' "

Those assembled continued in this strain, and constantly expressed themselves as opposed to the law, and their determination to resist its execution. They boasted that every

man in Northampton county would assist them except a few
tories, and that between Quakertown and the Delaware, they
could raise ten thousand men; and further that General Washington had sent them word that he had twenty thousand men
to assist them. Some spoke in German and others in English.
After John Freis took Mr. Childs into the house, he left him
among the crowd and went out again, being gone some time.
When he returned he apologized to him for the manner in
which his men had used him. He then took him into an inner room where there were but few people, and demanded his
assessment papers. He gave him some papers he had about
him, but which did not refer to the collection of taxes, when
Fries gave a shout and told his men he had got what they
wanted. He then went out of the room, most of his men following him. The crowd were gone but a short time when
they returned without Fries, shouting, and rushed up to Childs
and took hold of him. Some were armed with clubs, guns,
pistols, &c., and others had swords. Daniel Weidner, whose
house he had assessed in the morning, was with them, who insisted upon Childs surrendering to him the assessment he had
made of his house, but he did not give it up. They again
took hold of him and shook him severely; and one man came
forward and said he should be shot. Conrad Marks was present armed with a sword, who made many threats, but did not
attempt to put any of them into execution. Childs attempted
to reason with them, but it had little if any effect toward pacifying them. During this proceeding, Fries returned into the
room and gave back the papers to Childs, telling him at the
same time he must now go home, and never come back again
into the township to assess, or he would be shot. To this he
replied that he had left the township with a view of not returning to it again unless compelled to do so by authority, and
that, from their present treatment, as he would never be likely
to come back without such authority, they might have leave
to shoot him. They then told him they wished him and Mr.
Foulke to inform the government what had been done, as soon
as they pleased. After a little more parleying they gave him
his liberty, when he rode off, glad enough to make his escape
from such unpleasant company.

There is some discrepance, as regards what took place at Quakertown the day the assessors were captured, between the records of the transaction and the relation of those who have a recollection of the event. We had interviews with some of the oldest inhabitants of that section upon the subject, and find them at variance with the testimony drawn from other sources. They state that the assessors were chased to Quakertown by Fries and his party, and that he snapped his gun three times at Mr. Foulke; that the latter sprang from his horse at the porch of Enoch Roberts' tavern and ran in, when they hid him in the cellar, where he remained concealed until ten o'clock, when he was released and ran home. Another version has it that he was hid under the counter in the bar-room, and that Fries hunted all through the house, but was unable to find him; that they got Fries, Haney and Getman drunk, when Foulke stole out and went home. Still another story is that he was kept confined in a stable, and that Mr. Childs was sent to inform his wife, but was afraid to go into the house, and walked in the yard until ten o'clock at night, when Foulke came home. These statements differ so widely, from the evidence given on the trial, we have thought it best to follow the testimony, believing that to be the nearest correct, because it was related under oath soon after the events happened. One circumstance is told by those who remember the difficulty, which seems so reasonable it is probably true; that a man named Everhart pointed his gun at Foulke, while they had him imprisoned at the tavern, but was so drunk he fell over while doing so. They afterward examined the gun, and found that the ball had been put in the bottom, and the powder on top.

The circumstances which took place at Quakertown decided the assessors to make no further attempt to take assessments in Milford, as they were convinced it would lead to difficulty, and, possibly, bloodshed. In other parts of the county the law was quietly acquiesced in, and the officers discharged their duty peaceably, but it was, nevertheless, very unpopular and odious. For the time being, Fries and his friends had prevented the execution of the law in the disaffected district, but as far as we have been able to learn, no public outrages were committed, and their only desire seemed to be to prevent the officers, by intimidation, from making the assessments.

The foregoing embraces the proceedings of the insurrectionists, or insurgents, while opposing the execution of the house tax law in Milford. It will be noticed their whole conduct was of that earnest character which marks the actions of men who are sincere in what they are doing. While there was, naturally, considerable noise and confusion attendant upon their conduct, and high excitement prevailing, there was no unnecessary disturbance, and nothing that can properly be called violence. Rude they were, but not to an extent to create a breach of the peace. We have every reason to believe they considered the law of the most oppressive character, and their minds had probably been inflamed against it by the misrepresentation of others. This opinion had been formed before they had an opportunity to learn its provisions and operations, and they were afterward either too much prejudiced, or their pride would not permit them, to be rightly informed. The law of itself was a mild one, and no one who examines it at this day can see anything in it to cause such opposition to it. The rates were light, and the burden of the tax fell upon the shoulders of those who were the best able to bear it. There was likewise a public necessity for that or a similar Act of Congress, and it was necessary that the revenue should be increased, as there was every probability of the government being driven into a war with one of the most powerful nations of Europe. The situation of the politics of the country had something to do with the opposition that was raised against the law. But recently, before their passage, the two statutes known as the Alien and Sedition Laws had passed Congress, which were received with a burst of indignation that had never been equaled in the country. They brought the administration of Mr. Adams into great unpopularity, if not detestation. The odium that rested upon these laws was reflected upon the house tax, and thus it was condemned in advance because it was found in bad company. Many honest people believed that an Act of Congress taxing the country, emanating from the same government which had given them the Alien and Sedition Laws, must naturally be a wicked one, and, they were so well convinced of this, they were not open to persuasion to the contrary. Another circumstance, in connection with the manner in which the law was executed, had something to do with its great unpopularity. The officers exceeded their duties, and went beyond their instructions. The assessors were only required, by law, to assess the *houses*, *lands* and *slaves*, and were not directed to count the window lights of the houses, which was a duty superadded by the officers who had charge of affairs. The fact of the window lights being counted created suspicion in the minds of the people that it was done for the purpose of making them the subject of future taxation. This, more than anything else, led to the meetings held by the people, and, notwithstanding the unpopularity of the measure, there would probably never have been any "insurrection" or outbreak, had the assessors confined themselves to the duties which the law required of them. The abuse of the law had probably more to do with causing the disturbance than the law itself.

# The Fries Rebellion.

## CHAPTER IV.

### Opposition to the House Tax Law in Northampton.

Having recounted, in the preceeding chapter, the opposition to the House Tax Law in Bucks county, and the disturbance growing out of it, we shall now proceed to show what took place in Northampton.

It will be remembered that Jacob Eyerley was appointed commissioner for a district composed of the counties of Northampton,[1] Luzerne[2] and Wayne.[3] As soon as the law was passed, the people of Northampton manifested so much opposition to it, Commissioner Eyerley believed there would be difficulty in carrying it out. This was before he had entered upon the discharge of his duties. While at Reading, in October, he was informed by the commissioner from Bucks, that he had seen persons who had traveled through that county, and in every tavern he stopped at, the law was the subject of general conversation and denunciation, and great pains were taken to find the friends of government, in order to pursuade them not to accept the office of assessor. In consequence of this feeling there was great difficulty in finding suitable persons for these appointments. He selected one in each township, taking the most suitable for the duties, from all the in-

---

[1] Northampton county was cut off from Bucks, 1752.

[2] Luzerne county was cut off from Northumberland, by Act of September 25, 1786, and so named in honor of the Chevelier De la Luzerne, then French Minister to the United States. Its original territory embraced 5000 square miles, but its present area is but 1427. A portion of the celebrated Wyoming Valley lies within it.

[3] Wayne county was organized by the Act of March 21, 1798, out of a portion of Northampton, and named after General Anthony Wayne. The original area was 1300 square miles.

formation he could get. Commissions were immediately sent them, with notice to meet the commissioner to receive instructions. At that time the commissioner did not believe the state of things was as bad in Northampton as he afterward found it to be. The disaffection in Bucks had spread over the line into some of the neighboring townships of the adjoining county, and the people had become as hostile to the tax as Fries and his neighbors.

Commissioner Eyerley divided Northampton into three districts and first met the assessors November 3, at Nazareth[4]. Two were absent, and some of those present asked to be excused from serving, on account of the hostility of the people and the assessors fear of injury. As the commissioner had no authority to relieve them they were not excused. Finding them misinformed of the nature and operation of the law the commissioner took great pains to disabuse their minds, and, with such success, they consented to serve, and were given instructions. The following day he met the assessors of the second district at Allentown,[5] all being present but one. The same difficulty met him here he had to contend with at Nazareth, disinclination to accept for the same reason, opposition of the people to the law, and fear of being assaulted, should they attempt to make the assessments. With a good deal of difficulty those present were induced to accept the appointments. As it was taken for granted the absent assessor, a Mr. Horne, did not intend to accept, a blank commission was left with Mr. Balliott, a prominent resident of the county, with authority to appoint some suitable man in place of Mr. Horne. The assessors of the first district were met November 6, in Chestnut Hill township, with two absentees.

---

[4] Nazareth, a village of a few hundred inhabitants, in Northampton county, ten miles from Bethlehem, was founded by the Moravians, 1775. The first house erected was a spacious stone mansion for the residence of Count Zingendorf. The building was converted into a school, 1785, and, from that time, known as "Nazareth Hall," a celebrated boarding school for boys.

[5] Allentown was laid out by James Allen, 1762, after whom it was named, and called Northampton until 1838, when the present name was adopted. It is the county seat of Lehigh, and situated on the right bank of the Lehigh river. It is one of the most beautiful inland cities in the State.

One of these was a Mr. Kearne, of Easton,[a] but as it was not convenient for him to accept, he named a Mr. Snyder, who was only commissioned. He met with the others the same day; accepted the appointment and served. He stated there was much opposition to the law in his section of the county, and he did not understand it very well himself, but would do the best he could. The commissioner took considerable pains to explain the provisions of the law, which entirely satisfied him. He now became quite warm in its favor, and said he would ride fifty miles if it were necessary to accept the appointment, since he had been wrongly informed, about the law in the first place. The assessor from Hamilton township did not seem willing to accept his appointment, and it required a good deal of explanation and persuasion to overcome his disinclination. He at last consented, however, accepted his commission, and received his instructions.

In Northampton county the principal part of the opposition to the law was in the townships of Heidelberg, Weisenberg, Lynn, Low Hill, Penn, Moore, Upper Milford and Hamilton. In four districts it was of such violent character the law was not executed until after the troops were marched into them, and, in some of them, the people were almost unanimous against it. In Moore township, the opposition was only among a portion of the inhabitants, and, when the assessor was opposed when making the assessment, he called a town meeting and took the sense of the people. The assessor of Penn township did not meet the commissioners, but refused to accept the appointment in view of the difficulties in his way. Some time elapsed before any one could be found willing to accept the office, but, finally, one bold enough to assume the responsibility, presented himself and he was commissioned and qualified. When the people of the township

---

[a] Easton, the seat of justice of Northampton county, situated at the confluence of the Delaware and Lehigh, at what was known as "Forks of Delaware," was laid out by William Parsons, 1752. A ferry was established here as early as 1739, by David Martin, of Trenton, N. J., at which time a few log houses were standing on the present site of the town. A jail was completed, 1755, and the first court house erected, 1766. Easton has been the county seat since the organization of the county, 1752. It is the seat of Lafayette College, chartered, 1826.

heard that another person had been appointed in place of the one first named, and had undertaken to discharge the duties of the office, they became very violent and threatened him with personal injury. The leaders of the opposition collected a number of the disaffected into a mob, who waited upon the assessor, and gave him to understand harm would be done him if he attempted to take the rates. This demonstration intimidated him to such degree he resigned, and declined to have anything more to do with it. The hostility to the law continued so great in this township, the assessments were not made until sometime late in the spring of 1799, and after the presence of a military force had completely quelled everything like opposition.

The spirit of insubordination first manifested itself a little while before the general election, when meetings were held in different parts of the county to take action upon the subject. At one of these meetings the officers of the militia were invited to be present, and their co-operation, as the leaders of the military of the country, was earnestly desired. The leading object was to nominate candidates opposed to the law. At this meeting several resolutions were passed, one recommending the circulation of petitions asking a repeal of the Alien and Sedition Laws and the land tax. The proceedings were published in the newspapers and circulated among the people. A petition was given to each of the captains of militia to get signers. On the day of election the people turned out very generally, and, in most of the districts, the opposition to the government was so general, its friends dare not say a word in its favor for fear of being abused. The anti-administration candidates were elected by considerable majorities, and the people, generally, rejoiced at their success.

In Hamilton township, the people were so much enraged at Nicholas Michael, the assessor, for accepting the appointment, they went in large numbers to his house at night to do him bodily injury, but, being informed of their intention, he sought safety in flight. The next day he went to the commissioner and made complaint of the treatment he had received, tendered his resignation, and begged its acceptance. This was declined; he was told to return to his duty, and he would be protected in the discharge of it. He accompanied the commissioner to Easton, to see Mr. Sitgreaves, the United States Attorney for the district, before whom he intended to make affidavit in order to have some of the evil-disposed placed under arrest. Mr. Sitgreaves not being at home, they went to Judge Traill,[7] an associate judge of the county; but, when they arrived there, Michael became alarmed and begged to be allowed until the next morning to consider the matter; saying, that if he informed against the people, he and his family would be ruined. In the morning he wished to be put in jail to be kept from danger, so great were his fears, but his request was not complied with.

In the present state of excitement the commissioner deemed it advisable to call a public meeting, at which the people could come together and have the law explained to them, as he was of opinion, the greater part of the opposition arose from a misconception of its provisions. With this object in view, he gave Mr. Michael a letter to take to the constable of the township, requesting him to fix the time and place for the meeting, and to give proper and timely notice thereof. Mr. Eyerley promised to be present to explain the law to such as did not understand it. The constable, accordingly, announced the meeting to be held at the public house of a Mr. Heller, and the time fixed was a few days before New Year's, but we have not been able to ascertain the precise day. The commissioner was present according to promise, being accom-

---

[7] Robert Traill was born on one of the Orkney Islands, April 29, 1744, and was the son of a clergyman. He came to America, 1763, reaching Philadelphia the 25th of December. He shortly went to Easton where he was occupied in a store, taught school a year; then studied law, and was admitted to the bar, 1777. He took an active part in the Revolution, and was Secretary of the County Committee of Safety from 1776 to 1778; was appointed a justice of the peace, 1777, and military storekeeper at Easton, March 11, 1778. He was sheriff of the county from 1781 to 1784; member of the Assembly for the sessions of 1785-86; member of the Supreme Executive Council of Pennsylvania, 1786-88; and was commissioned one of the Associate Judges of Northampton, holding the office from May 14, 1796, to January 22, 1798, when he resigned. Judge Traill died at Easton, July 31, 1816. He filled a large space in public estimation, exerted a wide influence and was distinguished for his probity of character. His descendants, in the female line, live at Easton, one of them being Dr. Traill Green.

panied into the township by William Henry,[a] one of the Associate Judges of Northampton. When they arrived at the place of meeting they found some seventy persons assembled, among them three or four in uniform, whose arms were stacked behind the tavern door. After the meeting was organized, Mr. Eyerley arose and stated that he had come there as their friend, to explain the house tax law, that they might no longer be in ignorance of its provisions. He and Judge Henry then proceeded to explain the statutes as they understood them, but with little effect, as the people were not disposed to listen to any explanation that would be likely to give them a more favorable opinion of the odious law. They hated it, and did not wish to think well of it. In order to reconcile the people, to the assessment of the rates, he proposed they should elect an assessor of their own; this they refused to do, saying, if they did, it would amount to submission to the law, which they did not mean to make. The assessor already appointed was anxious to resign, but this he was not allowed to do, as no one could be found who would accept the appointment in his place.

In Upper Milford,[b] the people opposed to the law held a township meeting and appointed a committee of three to wait upon the assessor when he should begin the assessment, and request him to desist; and about the last of December, when he began the work, he was met by this committee and informed he could not proceed. No violence was offered, but he was given to understand he would not be permitted to carry out the law. He immediately wrote the commissioner

---

[a] William Henry, son of William and Ann Henry, was born at Lancaster, Pa., March 12, 1757. In 1778 he engaged in the manufacture of fire-arms in Northampton county, and in 1808 erected a forge in which the first iron manufactured in the county was drawn March 9, 1809. In 1813 he built the Boulton Gun Works on the Bushkill, which are still continued by his descendants of the name. Mr. Henry was commissioned January 14, 1788, a justice of the peace and Judge of the Courts of Common Pleas and Quarter Sessions of the county. He resigned 1814. In 1792 he was elected one of the Presidential electors of the State and cast his vote for Washington for President. He removed to Philadelphia, 1818, where he died April 21, 1821.

[b] Upper Milford, a township of Lehigh county, but originally in Bucks until Northampton was cut off, was organized, 1738. There were two Milfords, Upper and Lower, the former falling in Northampton on the division of Bucks, 1752. Germans settled here in the first quarter of the last century.

informing him of the situation of affairs, and asked advice as to the course to be pursued. The latter again thought it advisable to have a public meeting called, at which he would make another effort to explain the law to the people, and endeavor to satisfy them with its provisions. He directed the assessor to give notice to John Schymer, Moretz and other leading men of the township, that he would meet them at such time and place as they might appoint. The place fixed upon was the house of Mr. Schymer, date not known. When the time arrived the commissioner set out for the place of meeting, accompanied by Judge Henry, and, when he arrived within four miles of it, he was met by a friend who advised him not to attend, saying the people were so violent his life would be endangered, but he disregarded the warning and kept on. He found some 75 men assembled at the house of Schymer, several of them having French cockades in their hats, showing very plainly which side they took in politics.

One of the petitions, which a previous meeting had recommended should be circulated for signatures, was handed the commission who read it to the people. Some of them, upon hearing it, said it was not such a petition as they had been led to believe it was, as it mentioned nothing about the stamp act. As there was a report in circulation that the act was not in force, Mr. Eyerley read it in German, and explained to them it was their duty to submit to it. One, George Shaeffer, denying that it was a law, the question was submitted to the decision of Mr. Schymer, who, being a justice of the peace, had considerable influence over the minds of the people. Shaeffer was inclined to be noisy and created a disturbance, and he and others used abusive language to the assessor, Mr. Heckewelder,[10] accusing him, among other things, of having been a tory during the Revolution. Mr. Eyerley proposed that inasmuch as they were opposed to the present assessor, he would give them the privilege of electing one of their own number, to whom he would give the appointment. This they declined,

---

[10] Heckewelder, who lived at Emaus, now in Lehigh county, was appointed one of the assessors for Upper Milford or Salisbury, probably the latter. He was doubtless a son, or grandson, of Heckewelder, the Moravian divine.

saying: "We will do no such thing; if we do, we at once acknowledge that we submit to the law, and that is what we will not do." Three of the Shaeffers made demonstrations to beat Heckewelder, but were deterred by the interference of others, and he was allowed to go away without injury. The commissioner, even with the countenance of Mr. Schymer and several other well disposed persons present, found it impossible to reconcile the multitude to the law, and he returned home a second time without having effected anything. The opposition to the law in this township, likewise, was not overcome until the presence of troops intimidated them into submission, when the rates were taken without further trouble.

Resistance to the enforcement of the law had now reached that stage it became necessary for the authorities to take some notice of it. About January 15, 1799, Judge Henry, at the request of Commissioner Eyerley, and upon complaint of the assessors that they found it impossible to proceed in the execution of their duty, issued a number of subpœnas to bring persons, cognizant of the opposition to the execution of the laws, before him that he might make a careful examination of the cause of complaint and ascertain its truth. The witnesses who appeared were generally very reluctant to give information, being afraid the insurgents would do them some injury. The Judge made appointment to meet a number of persons at Trexlertown," to inquire further into the matter, and a considerable crowd assembled. Among those present was part of a company of light horse under Captain Jarrett.[12] The men were mostly in uniform, and many of them noisy and impudent. The Judge was attended by the commissioner and Mr. Balliott. They, who were present, paid little respect to the officers but ridiculed, and made fun of them. From the indications at this meeting, it was evident the disturbance could not be quelled by the local officers, and it was thought best to

---

[11] Trexlertown, in Lehigh county, but, at that time, in Northampton, is a small post village, eight miles from Allentown, on the Catasauqua and Fogelsville railway. It is in a rich agricultural region.

[12] Although Captain Jarrett was evidently a man of some prominence in the community, we have not been able to obtain any information concerning him beyond that found in the text. The company he commanded was a local volunteer organization. Henry Jarrett, probably a relative, commanded a troop of light horse at Marcus Hook, 1814.

appeal to the Federal authority. The steps now about to be taken changed the aspect of affairs. Hitherto, it was considered but a local disaffection to a law of questionable expediency, and improperly understood, and which, in due time, would subside and be heard of no more. Down to this point it had hardly attracted public attention outside of the rural districts where the opposition was made, and neither State nor Federal Government had given it consideration. It now assumed National importance, and what shortly before, was unworthy the attention of politicians or statesmen, became a matter of great moment. The action of Judge Henry was the incipient step that changed the affair to an insurrection, and converted the opponents of the house-tax law into insurgents and traitors to their country.

Mr. Sitgreaves, United States District Attorney, was sent a number of the depositions he had caused to be taken to Judge Peters,[13] of the United States District Court, Philadelphia. This was some time in February, and the first official information the Judge received on the subject, although he had before heard of it as a matter of news. He examined a few witnesses in addition to the affidavits, and, from the facts elicited, thought it his duty to issue warrants for the parties. Being much engaged he directed the District Attorney to draw up the form of warrants for his approval and signature. It had been decided, that, in order to ease the minds of the people, the warrants should be drawn in the nature of an order for the defendant to appear before some justice of the peace, or judge of the county, and give bail for appearance at the Circuit Court of the United States, but circumstances prevented it. After this had been decided upon, it came to the knowledge of the authorities that several of the magistrates themselves were disaffected, and others were prevented doing their duty through fear of injury. The Judge also had scruples as to the legality of the measure, whether persons, arrested on his warrants, could be taken before an inferior magistrate While his

---

[13] Richard Peters was born in Philadelphia, 1744; admitted to the bar, 1763; appointed a Justice of the United States District Court for the Eastern District of Pennsylvania, 1792, and died on the Bench, 1828, after continued service of 36 years.

mind was in doubt, he received additional information of the state of the people in the disaffected districts, and this induced him, both to make a change in the form of the warrants and the procedure under it. The warrants were now to be made returnable to Judge Peters' Court.

## The Fries Rebellion.

### CHAPTER V.

#### The Marshal Makes Arrests in Northampton.

When the form of the warrants was agreed upon, they were made out and put into the hands of Colonel Nichols,[1] United States Marshal, to be served. This was about January 25, and the Marshal was directed to proceed to Northampton county immediately and make the arrests. He left Philadelphia on the 26th, serving a few subpœnas on the road, in order to collect evidence, reaching Nazareth on March 1st. Here the Marshal met Commissioner Eyerley, and told him of the object of his visit, requesting him to go with him to serve the warrants executed. Those placed in his hands being only for the arrest of persons in Northampton county. The next morning, accompanied by Eyerley, and Eyerman, the Marshal set out to execute the warrants. They went first into Lehigh township, where twelve were arrested, all against whom they had process, but five others came in afterward and gave themselves up. Their offence being resistance to the execution of the house-tax law. They then returned to Bethlehem, where they were met by Colonel Balliott.

The Marshal's party next went to Macungie township, where they had no difficulty until they came to the house of George Snyder, near Emaus,[2] on whom the Marshal wished to serve a subpœna. Snyder and his wife used abusive

---

[1] Samuel Nichols was appointed U. S. Marshal of Pennsylvania, April 10, 1795; qualified May 18th, and confirmed June 26th. He served one term of four years; was reappointed during a recess of the Senate, June 26th, 1799, and succeeded, Dec. 6th, 1799, by John Hall. The State had not yet been divided into two districts. His county is not given.

[2] Emaus is a small town, lying at the foot of South Mountain, five miles southeast of Allentown, on the East Penn. railroad. The Moravians organized a church here, 1747, the house in which they worshipped being built as early as 1742.

(48)

language toward them, the woman taking the lead. The husband came out of his house with a club, and positively refused to receive the subpœna. He called the Marshal and the men with him rascals and highway robbers, and, upon being told he was only wanted to go to Philadelphia as a witness, he refused with an oath. The Marshal finding he could do nothing with him requested Daniel Swartz's son to read and explain the subpœna to him, and leaving it with him to be served if it were possible. Thence they proceeded to Millarstown,³ a few miles' distant. On the road they stopped at the house of the Rev. Mr. VanBuskirk,⁴ where they left their horses and walked into the town. The Marshal had a warrant for George Shaeffer, active in opposing the law, and to whose house they next proceeded to arrest him, but he was not at home. Not meeting with success in this case they went to the tavern, where a considerable number of people had assembled.

They now made an attempt to arrest a man named Shankwyler, who also lived in Millarstown. The Marshal and Commissioner walked over to his house, leaving Mr. Eyerman at

---

³ Millarstown, now called Macungie, signifying "the feeding place of bears," and laid out by Peter Millar about 1776, is situated at the foot of South Mountain on the East Penn. railroad, nine miles from Allentown. It was incorporated in 1857.

⁴ Jacob VanBuskirk, a native of Holland, settled with his family on a tract he purchased in Lower Macungie township, Lehigh county, November 19, 1784. The borough of Macungie now occupies the same land. I do not know the maiden name of his wife, but she was a sister of the great-grandmother of the late General Hartranft. He preached for the Lehigh Church at Germantown, and at the Trappe, visiting his congregations on horseback. He built, and, for several years operated, the tannery at Macungie, owned by his great-grandson, James Singmaster. He had three sons and four daughters; George became a physician, and settled at Pottstown; Jacob removed to New York State, where he died; John, the third son, settled in Virginia, afterward came to Philadelphia and kept an hotel. He married a Miss Eckhart, of Berks county. Of the daughters, Lydia married Adam Singmaster, of Millarstown, and, after his death, Daniel Good, of Upper Milford; another married John Shimer, of Shimersville, Northampton county, E. S. Shimer, Mayor of Allentown, being a grand-son. Mr. VanBuskirk was an ardent supporter of John Adams' Administration, and, during the excitement of the "Fries Rebellion," 1798, an attempt was made on his life. While sitting at home, surrounded by his family, a bullet was sent crashing through the window, but he luckily escaped injury. He was buried at North Wales, and his wife at the Lehigh Church. Adam Singmaster, who married the daughter Lydia, was a descendant, probably a son, of John Adam Zangmiester, who came from Wurtumburg in the good ship, "Patience," Hugh Steelmaster, September 19, 1749, and settled in Bucks county. Adam, when a young man, went to Millarstown, where he obtained employment in Rev. Jacob VanBuskirk's family, and afterward married the daughter.

the tavern. They had not intimated they desired to arrest him, but when they left the tavern the people suspected their intention and followed them in a crowd to the number of about fifty. They went in advance of the officers, and, reaching the house before them, filled the large room. When the Marshal arrived a friend pointed out Shankwyler to Col. Nichols, but observing what was going on, he withdrew into the crowd, with the intention of hiding himself from view; but the Marshal followed him, and, putting his hand upon his shoulder, informed him he was a prisoner, in the name of the United States, announcing himself as the United States Marshal for the Eastern District of Pennsylvania. Shankwyler, having no idea of being captured without some resistance, broke loose from the Marshal and fled toward the barn. He proclaimed he would not injure the Marshal, but made threats against Eyerley and Balliott, toward whom he manifested great hostility. The people became much excited at this proceeding, and many cried out in German, "Strike! Strike!" Some said if he were taken out of his house they would fight as long as they had a drop of blood in their bodies. They seemed inclined to lay violent hands upon Balliott, and one of the crowd presumed to pull the cockade from his hat. The Marshal warned them of the consequences of their attempting to strike, and reasoned with them upon their riotous conduct. Finding that himself and companions were in danger, the Marshal unbuttoned his coat, that the people might see a pair of pistols he had with him, and also in order that he might be able to grasp them quickly, should he find it necessary to use them. The determined manner of the Marshal had its effect, and the crowd became quieter. Shankwyler refused to accompany the Marshal to Bethlehem, and swore he would resist the authorities of the United States, let the consequences be what they might. He was told such a course would ruin himself and family, and be the destruction of his property, to which he replied that his father had fought against the stamp act, and he would resist the tax law which was supported by none but tories and the friends of government. At last he was prevailed upon to promise to meet the Marshal at Bethlehem, but could not be induced to say that he would submit or surrender himself. Seeing that nothing further could be accomplished there, the officers took their leave. As they left the house the people set up a shout and hurrahed for "Liberty." The Marshal now continued on his rounds. He procured a constable to show him where Adam Stephen, Herman Hartman, and Daniel Everly, for whom he had warrants, lived. Having arrested these persons he and his party returned to Bethlehem, where they arrived on the evening of March 6. Bethlehem was his headquarters, and here he had his prisoners confined.

Bethlehem, the place of confinement of the Marshal's prisoners, was such an important point at that day it will not do to pass it by with a mere mention of its name, but deserves something more. It stands on the north bank of the Lehigh, Northampton county, twelve miles above where the river empties into the Delaware. Here was made the first permanent settlement of the Moravians in North America. The first tree was felled on the spot where Bethlehem stands Dec. 22, 1740, by a small party from Nazareth. The cold was intense, the snow lay deep on the ground; and through the winter they encountered many privations and hardships. By the opening of spring a small log house was completed. On September 8, 1741, the corner-stone of a second, and much more commodious, house, was laid with interesting religious ceremonies. The first house stood until 1823, when it was torn down to make room for the Eagle Hotel stables; but the second has weathered the storms of nearly one hundred and sixty years, and still stands as a monument of the founding of Bethlehem. The first tree to build the first house was cut down by David Nitschman, who was born in Moravia, September 18, 1676, and died at Bethlehem, April 14, 1758. He was the first bishop of the brethren in America, and officiated at the laying of the corner-stone of the second building in 1741.

A recent writer speaking of this interesting building says: "Here, as in a common home, lived, side-by-side, the artisan and man of leisure—a little company met together from the various walks of life, self-denying and devoted men, actuated by one spirit, and that the spirit of mutual love for Christ. Here lived for a number of years the elders of the congregation, its bishops and ministers. Here they met in conference to deliberate on the condition of the Lord's work in their midst, and abroad among the Indian tribes. Its walls have echoed to the voice of Zinzendorf,[5] and, for fifteen years was the home of that great and good man, the worthy Bishop Spangenberg.[6] In the little hall on the second floor, the place of worship for the congregation as late as 1751, Spangenberg presided on two occasions at interviews with deputations from the rude tribes of Wyoming Valley.[7] Nanticokes and Shawnese, dressed in all their savage finery of feathers and painted deerskin, had come to see the home of the intrepid missionary, whose lonely canoe they had encountered on the upper waters of the Susquehanna, to smoke the friendly pipe, and assure him of their good-will in a covenant of peace and mutual friendship."

[5] Count Zinzendorf, founder of the Moravian Colony north of the Lehigh, and descended of a noble Austrian family, was born at Dresden, Saxony, May 26, 1700. He was educated ar Halle and the University of Wittenberg, and afterward spent some time in traveling. He was married in 1732 to the Countess Von Reuss, and became a convert to the Moravian faith shortly afterward. He landed at New York, December 2, 1741, reaching Philadelphia the 10th, and Bethlehem the 24th. He immediately became an object of general interest and was recognized as the head of the Moravian movement lately initiated in the province. In June, 1742, he organized the Moravian congregation at Bethlehem, and preached his farewell sermon at Philadelphia, December 31, leaving the same evening for New York to embark for Europe, where he died May 9, 1760. He was accompanied to America by his daughter Benigna.

[6] Augustus Gottlieb Spangenberg, a bishop of the Unitas Fratrum, or Moravian Church, was born at Klettenberg, Prussia, July 15, 1704, and died at Bershelsdorf, Saxony, September 18, 1792. He graduated at Jena, where he later became a professor, and also at Halle. In 1735 he led the first Moravian colonists to Georgia. Having been appointed to preside over the Moravian Churches in America, he was raised to the episcopalcy in 1744 and arrived at Bethlehem, Pa., the same year. In 1760 he was recalled to Europe to take a seat in the Supreme Board of the Church over which body he presided twenty-three years. He may justly be called the founder of the Moravian Church in America. He was a learned theologian, a man of great power, and a writer of many historical and theological works.

[7] The Wyoming Valley, so famous in history and song, lies along the Susquehanna, and spreads about Wilkesbarre, the county seat of Luzerne. In it took place the bloody massacre of its inhabitants by Indians, in 1778, and avenged in 1779 by an army under General Sullivan. Campbell's "Gertrude of Wyoming" has made this valley almost as famous as the Vale of Cashmers.

Bethlehem was originally intended as a place of rendezvous for the missionaries among the Delaware and Mohican Indians, which it held for twenty years, but, at the end of that time, became the seat of the Moravian congregation, organized by Count Zinzendorf. A school for girls was opened as early as 1749, but the boarding school was not commenced until 1785, and is still in operation.

During the Revolutionary War Bethlehem was often visited by American troops, and upon more than one occasion the brethren were sufferers from military exactions. On the retreat of Washington through New Jersey, December, 1776, Lee's divison, under the command of General Sullivan, after crossing the Delaware, came to this place, where it encamped on the 17th, and La Fayette spent some time there to recover from the wound received at Brandywine.

In the spring of 1778, the single Sisters presented to Count Pulaski an elegant embroidered banner, which was borne at the head of his regiment until he fell at Savannah, 1779. Bethlehem was also visited by the Baron De Kalb, September, 1777. Hospitals were established there for the sick and wounded of the army, and it was also made a depot for provisions; and, in fact, during the whole war it was an important point in military operations. Washington styled the weaving department of Sisters House, "the first domestic manufactories of the land," and from there supplied himself and wife with articles of wearing apparel.

The situation of Bethlehem is beautiful and romantic in the extreme, and nature and art combined have rendered it one of the most charming spots in the country. It has grown into a town of some 10,000 inhabitants, and become an important business centre. Two railroads and a canal give the inhabitants great facilities for trade, and manufactories are rapidly growing up around it. The influx of strangers has done away with much of the exclusive Moravian impress formerly stamped upon the town, but the spirit of their institutions still prevails to a great extent, and may be said to be the governing influence.

The arrest of the persons for whom warrants were issued, and their confinement at Bethlehem by the Marshal, caused unusual excitement throughout the country. It created great indignation in the disaffected districts of Northampton and Bucks, and was considered an act of tyranny and oppression on the part of the government. As soon as it became known the arrests were made, the leaders of the opposition to the law determined to rescue them, if possible. For the purpose of consulting on the subject, a meeting was called at the public house of Conrad Marks*, Milford, Bucks county, on March 7. Notices were carried around the evening before and left at the houses of those known to be friendly to the movement. By ten o'clock a number of people had assembled, and considerable excitement was manifested. The general sentiment was in favor of immediate organization and marching to Bethlehem to take the prisoners from the hands of the Marshal. The crowd was formed in a company, and John Fries elected captain. They were variously armed; some with guns, others with swords and pistols, while those with less belligerent feelings, carried clubs. Subsequently, when Fries was examined before Judge Peters, he said his "motive in going to Bethlehem to rescue the prisoners was not from personal attachment, or regard for any of the persons who had been arrested, but proceeded from a general aversion to the law, and an intention to impede and prevent its execution." This reason, however, hardly explains their course, under the circumstances. Their plan was first to march to Millarstown and thence to Bethlehem.

The people of Northampton, meanwhile, had also taken action in reference to a rescue of the prisoners. A meeting to

---

* Conrad Marks' tavern was in Milford township, Bucks county, near where the four corners of Bucks, Montgomery, Berks and Lehigh come together. His petition for license, in the Quarter Sessions office, was to August term, 1796, in which he states he had removed to the well-known tavern on the Magunshey (Macungie) road in said township of Milford, formerly occupied by George Horlacker," also that the house had been "kept as such above forty years." His endorsers were David Spinner and George Horlacker. For many years the house was known as Geary's tavern.

consult on the subject was called at the tavern of Martin Ritter,⁹ to meet at 10 o'clock, on the morning of March 7. Notice was also given for two or three companies of light horse to meet there at the same time, one of which was commanded by Captain Jarrett."

At the hour appointed a considerable number of persons were on the ground, and much noise, confusion and excitement prevailed. Upon the meeting being organized, and a conference had about the matter, that had brought them together, it was unanimously resolved to march for Bethlehem without delay. The strength of the party which marched for that place we have no means of knowing, as the records do not give it. Soon after starting they selected a commander, the choice falling upon Andrew Shiffert. There were a few present who questioned the propriety of the movement, but the general voice was so nearly unanimous in its favor, their advice was not listened to. The excitement ran high, and the multitude clamored to be led to the rescue of their friends in the hands of the Federal authorities. They did not look at the consequences that might recoil upon themselves, nor did they care at that particular moment, for they were burning under a sense of real or imagined wrong. They were blind to the nature of the step they were taking, and deaf to the voice of reason. The multitude believed, in case they should succeed in rescuing the prisoners, the matter would end there. Or, if it did cross the minds of the most far-seeing that such indignity to the government might be taken notice of, and troops ordered there to capture the guilty, it was not supposed, for a moment, the authorities would be able to do anything with them. With this feeling the march was taken up for Gunes' tavern, three miles from Bethlehem, where some confederates

---

⁹ We are not able to fix the locality of Martin Ritter's tavern. We thought, at first, it was on the sight of the present Rittersville, four miles from Bethlehem, on the road to Allentown. But this was imposible as the place of meeting of the Northampton insurgents was on the south side of the Lehigh, while Rittersville is on the north.

¹⁰ The same Captain Jarrett previously mentioned. His military, on this occasion, was a regularly organized volunteer company.

were expected to join them. Here they resumed the march for the bridge that crosses the Lehigh at South Bethlehem."

---

[11] The South Bethlehem *Star*, published a few years ago, the following account of the establishing of a ferry and the subsequent building of a bridge across the Lehigh at Bethlehem, by which the insurgents crossed: " The first public means of crossing the Lehigh was a ferry at the same place where the old Lehigh bridge now crosses the river. It was opened on March 11, 1743, and the man who first paddled passengers across the new ferry was Adam Schaus. Ferriage was at first, for a horse and rider, 3d. In 1745 the use of the ferry was free to all who lived in Bethlehem or delt there. Travelers were expected to pay if they would, but in case they objected they were not to be constrained. Improvements gradually crept in and 1750 wharves were constructed. Eight years thereafter a rope was introduced which rendered a passage across the river a much less serious matter than heretofore. At last came a bridge in 1794. John Schropp, warden, was empowered by an Act of Assembly to undertake the enterprise and to associate stockholders with himself. That first bridge was built of hemlock, was uncovered and cost $7800. In 1816 this bridge was removed and a more substantial structure put in its place. The latter bridge was also uncovered. In April, 1827, the present Bethlehem Bridge Company was organized. In 1841 the second bridge across the Lehigh was swept away by a freshet, after which the present covered one was constructed. After the great freshet of 1862 the present bridge had to be partially rebuilt, a portion of it having been carried away by the waters."

**JUDGE WILLIAM HENRY**
OF NORTHAMPTON COUNTY.

# The Fries Rebellion.

## CHAPTER VI.

### Rescue of the Prisoners at Bethlehem.

Fries and his friends received word, the night before, that the Northampton people, opposed to the law, also intended to make an effort to take the prisoners from the hands of the Marshal. In the morning, Conrad Marks sent his son to Ritter's tavern, to learn what movement was on foot at that place. In the meantime the march was commenced for Millarstown, and when they had gone three or four miles on the road, young Marks was met returning. He informed them the Northampton people were already in motion, a large party having left Ritter's before his arrival; that it was not worth while for them to go, as a sufficient number was on the march to accomplish what they had in view. Upon learning this some were in favor of turning back, but Conrad Marks and John Fries advised they should go at least to Bethlehem to see what was going on there. The march was now resumed. Daniel Fries, son of John, says that his father started for Bethlehem mounted, but, when near old John Cline's, the animal cut its foot with the cork of his shoe and was disabled. Daniel was with him, and, as the horse was of no further service on the road, Fries sent his son back with it and continued the march on foot. They passed by Ritter's tavern, and followed the route of the Northampton contingent which had preceded them, overtaking and joining them at the south end of the bridge over the Lehigh at South Bethlehem.[1] The whole

---

[1] South Bethlehem is on the south bank of the Lehigh opposite Bethlehem. Here was the Crown Inn, the first licensed house on the Lehigh that rose to the dignity of a tavern, and on the site of it is the Union Railroad Station. The house was built in 1745 and licensed in June, 1746. The "Crown" played an important role in Colonial days. Around the site of this old hostelry has grown a town of fifteen thousand inhabitants; it is the seat of Lehigh University and here is located great iron works. Bethlehem and South Bethlehem are still connected by a wooden bridge that crosses the Lehigh at about the same place as the old one of '99.

command numbered about one hundred and forty men, including two companies of riflemen and one of mounted men, the latter being armed with broad swords. They presented quite a martial appearance. Their march through the thickly populated country swelled their ranks by the addition of a number, attracted by curiosity, who followed after to see what would take place, without any intention of taking part in the proceedings. They were neutrals.

We have already said the Marshal returned to Bethlehem with his prisoners the night of March 6, and confined them in the Sun tavern.[2] As the Marshal passed through the country, on his return, he heard a rumor that an attempt would be made to rescue the prisoners, but he did not conceive such a thing possible, supposing somebody, as a matter of amusement, had raised the story to alarm him. Upon reaching Bethlehem, however, the rumor was confirmed, and he was convinced a movement of the kind was on foot by a band of

---

[2] A public house has been kept on the spot where the Sun tavern stands for 140 years. The expediency of erecting a house of entertainment at Bethlehem was first considered and the location fixed upon, in July, 1754, but delay prevented its completion until 1758. Down to this time travelers were accommodated at "The Crown" on the south bank of the Lehigh, built 1743, and converted into a farm house in 1794. Chastellux, a French gentleman traveling in America near the close of the last century says of the "Sun:" "This tavern was built at the expense of the Society of Moravian Brethren whom it served as a magazine, and is very handsome, and spacious. The person who keeps it is only the cashier, and obliged to render an account to the administrators. As we had already dined we only drank tea, but ordered breakfast for the next morning at 10 o'clock." An English gentleman traveling in this country at that period also visited Bethlehem and put up at the Sun tavern. He afterward translated the work of Chastellux, and in it, makes the following note in reference to this tavern: "This inn for its external appearances, and its interior accommodations, is equal to the best of the large inns in England, which, indeed, it very much resembles in many respects. The first time I was in Bethlehem, in company with my friends, Major Pierce Butler, Mr. Thomas Elliott and Mr. Charles Pinckney, Carolina gentlemen, we remained here two or three days, and were constantly supplied with venison, moose, game, and the most delicious red and yellow bellied trout, the highest flavored wild strawberries, the most luxurious asparagus and the best vegetables, in short, I ever saw; and notwithstanding the difficulty of procuring good wine and spirits at that period throughout the continent, we were here regaled with rum and brandy, of the best quality, and exquisite old Port and Madeira." The present condition and appearance of the Sun tavern are in strong contrast compared with a century ago. It is excelled by few, if any, public house outside the large cities, and the accommodations are of the best. It is frequently alleged Lafayette put up at the Sun tavern, while recovering from the wound received at Brandywine, 1777, but this is an error. He occupied the house lately owned by Ambrose Rauch, on Main street, torn down 1872. The Marquis was driven in a carriage from Bristol, on the Delaware, to Bethlehem, a distance of sixty miles.

armed men. The prisoners arrested in Lehigh township were
released upon their own bonds, with good securities for their
appearance, but the others were held in custody.

The information, that an attempt at rescue would be made,
naturally gave the Marshal great uneasiness, and he proceeded
to take such steps as were deemed necessary to prevent it.
He held a consultation with Judge William Henry, Mr.
Eyerley, the commissioner, Mr. Balliott, Joseph Horsfield,[3]
a justice of the peace at Bethlehem, and General Brown.[4] He
had received instructions before leaving Philadelphia to call
out a *posse comitatus* in case it should be found necessary, but
was forbidden to use an armed force. He made a demand
upon Judge Henry for armed men, but as the latter had
received similar instructions, and there could not be found any
authority authorizing it, the requisition was refused. It was
therefore decided to call such force as they were authorized to
accept, and, accordingly, summoned a civil posse. Twenty men
were called from Bethlehem and Easton, but only eighteen
responded, arriving between ten and eleven in the forenoon.
We have not been able to get the names of all, but among
them were William Barnett, John Barnett, Christian Winters,
Christian Roths and Philip Schlaugh. The prisoners were removed upstairs to a room thought to be more secure. As
General Brown was a person of influence in the county, the
Marshal requested him to command at Bethlehem and lend
the assistance of his counsel, but he declined on account of
having been absent so long from his family. In the meantime an officer was sent to arrest a clergyman named Eyer-

---

[3] Joseph Horsfield was a prominent citizen of Northampton, and justice of the peace many years at Bethlehem. He was the youngest child of Timothy and Mary Horsfield, who settled in Long Island, 1749, and removed to Bethlehem, 1750. He married a niece of the celebrated Anthony Benezet, Philadelphia, whose mother was a great court beauty during the reign of Louis XIV. He was a witness on the trial of Fries for the prosecution. He died at Bethlehem, 1834, at the age of 84 years.

[4] General Brown was a descendant of an immigrant who settled at "Craig's Settlement," Allen township, Northampton county, about 1735. He was prominent in his generation, and played an important part in the county during the Revolutionary struggle. Robert Brown, of that section, was a prominent man of his day and an officer in the Continental army.

man[5] and one John Fox, both active in opposing the law, and who were thought to be too dangerous to go at large. They were taken and brought in without opposition. The proceeedings becoming known in the surrounding country, a large number of people came to witness a conflict, which, it was supposed, could not be avoided.

About eleven o'clock, a Mr. Dixon, who arrived from Emaus, informed the Marshal he had seen a number of persons assembled at Ritter's tavern, under arms, some mounted, others on foot, who were about to march for Bethlehem; and also saw others on the road. This was the first positive information that an armed party was actually coming to attempt a rescue of the prisoners. In about half an hour two men, one armed with a smooth bore gun, the other with a rifle, arrived at the Sun, dismounted in the yard, came quietly into the house, and placed themselves by the side of each other opposite the door. The Marshal, and some of the people who were collected, inquired the reason of their coming there armed, when, after some hesitation, they replied they "had come upon a shooting frolic." Upon being questioned as to what they intended to shoot, one of them evaded a reply by saying they wanted to see what was best for the country. They were then told to withdraw, and not appear in arms to obstruct the process of the United States. To this they replied they were freemen, and had a right to go where they pleased. They were supposed to be of the insurgent force, and, as they would probably come straggling in, it was thought best to secure them in detail. They were accordingly arrested, their arms taken from them, and they were taken up stairs and confined in a chamber. Shortly after three other mounted men arrived in uniform, at the head of whom was Shankwyler, who had refused to submit to an arrest the day before. The Marshal asked him if he had come to surrender himself, but he replied

---

[5] Among the prisoners released at Bethlehem was Jacob Eyerman, a clergyman residing in Hamilton township, Northampton county, recently arrived from Germany. He was one of the most active in stirring up opposition to the house tax law, only second in influence to John Fries, and continued to preach to his congregation until his tongue was silenced by arrest. After his release he fled to the State of New York, where he was arrested and brought back. He was tried, found guilty of conspiracy; sentenced to one year with a fine of $50, and to give security for one year for his good behavior.

he came to meet his accuser. They gave no indication of creating a disturbance and mingled peaceably with others assembled. Information was now brought in that there was an armed force at the Lehigh bridge, on the march for the tavern. A consultation was held, and it was deemed best to send a deputation down to hold a conference with them, to learn their intention. It was agreed to send a delegation of four upon this duty, two Federalists and two anti-Federalists. The men selected were John Mulhallon,[6] William Barnett, Christian Roths and Isaac Hartzell, gentlemen of standing and influence in the county. They received no particular instructions, and were only charged to prevail upon the armed force not to come into town.

The deputation rode down through the main street of Bethlehem, crossed the Lehigh to the south bank, and proceeded about a half mile beyond the bridge, where they met a party of armed horsemen, whom they learned were from the neighborhood of Millarstown. These belonged to the Northampton contingent. Upon inquiring for the commanding officer, they were told they had no officers but were all commanders. The committee then told them the object of their visit, and used every persuasion to induce them to relinquish their march to Bethlehem. They explained to them the probable consequences of the rash step they were about to take; that they would be resisting the laws of the United States in rescuing the prisoners, and the Government would surely punish them for it. All they said seemed to have but little or no effect. While Judge Mulhallon and Mr. Barnett were talking with these people in front, Christian Roths went toward the rear to use his influence in that quarter. One of the men said to him, "We don't know you;" whereupon he told them in reply, that whether they knew him or not, they would thank him for the advice he had given them. Another pointed his gun at him. This did not alarm Roths, who mildly said, "Little man, consider what you are about; don't be too much in a hurry." While they were holding this parley a company

---

[6] John Mulhallon, called "Judge" Mulhallon, and probably Associate Judge at one time, was appointed the first Prothonotary for Lehigh county, when it was cut off from Northampton.

of armed riflemen came up. They were likewise informed of the wish of the Marshal, but they gave it no more heed than the others.

The march of the insurgents was now resumed and they continued to the bridge where another halt was made. The committee here held another parley with them, endeavoring, by all possible means, to induce them not to go over into the town. They now said that the Marshal had two of their men prisoners, who had gone to Bethlehem under arms, and they intended to set them free. They appeared to be alarmed at the idea of the prisoners being taken to Philadelphia for trial. While admitting they should be punished, if they had done wrong, they must be tried in Northampton county. When the committee saw the insurgents were determined to proceed, they suggested it would be better to send three or four men over as a deputation to confer with the Marshal. To this they agreed, and three of their number were appointed to go. Afraid lest these men should also be made prisoners, they stipulated with William Barnett that he should return them safely. The two committees then crossed the river to Bethlehem, and together proceeded to the Sun tavern. They were taken before the Marshal and had a conference with him. Upon inquiring the reason of so many armed men coming there, they replied they came to prevent him taking the prisoners to Philadelphia to be tried. He told them that that could not be, and advised them to go to their companions and persuade them to return to their homes. They requested that the two men, who had been made prisoners in the morning, should be released, which was done and their arms delivered to them. As the committee had promised, they now returned with these men to the south side of the river to deliver them to their companions.

We last took leave of John Fries and his friends on their march from Conrad Marks' tavern by the way of Millarstown to Bethlehem. They were a little in the rear of the Northampton contingent, and arrived at the bridge while the committee of citizens were gone to the tavern with the men deputed to confer with the Marshal. They did not halt any length of time on the south bank of the river, but pushed across and continued on to the tavern, where the prisoners were confined. Meanwhile, the committee of conference, on the part of the, Marshal, had started on their return accompanied by the two released prisoners and their three friends. When they reached the lower part of the village, they met the force of John Fries marching up the main street. They stopped him to hold a parley, and endeavored to prevail upon him and his men not to continue their march up into the town; but they disregarded their appeal and said they were determined to go on. One of the men, supposed to have been Fries, said, "This is the third day that I am out. I had a fight yesterday, and I mean to have one to-day if they do not let the prisoners clear." They now resumed the march. The force consisted of two companies of riflemen, and one of mounted men, numbering in all about one hundred and forty. The horsemen marched two abreast armed with drawn swords. The footmen carried rifles, at a trail, in single file. One of the companies was commanded by a Captain Staeler, and wore tri-colored cockades on their hats. Fries marched in front of the riflemen and was apparently in command

The appearance of this large armed force, so close at hand, created great confusion and excitement, not only at the tavern but throughout the town. A conflict between them and the Marshal's posse was now thought inevitable. The inhabitants and strangers in the town flocked around the scene of action to watch the course of events. The Marshal had a force of less than twenty men to protect eighteen prisoners, who were merely placed in different rooms in the tavern, without being further restrained of their liberty. When the insurgents were known to be coming, the prisoners were told their friends were at hand prepared to take them away, but they did not wish to be rescued. The force arrived about 1 o'clock in the day; marched into the yard in front of the tavern; halted, the horsemen dismounting, and the riflemen passing around the house drew up in the rear of the horses and rested on their arms. The men kept well in ranks, and appeared to be under good control. The Marshal doubled his guard over the prisoners and stationed two at the bottom and two at the top of the stairs, armed with pistols. Fries went into the tavern, accompanied by two of his men, and requested the sentinel at the foot of the stairway to let him go up to see the Marshal. Word was sent up to Colonel Nichols, who came forward and told the guard to let Captain Fries pass up. When he came to the Marshal, Fries informed him he had come for the prisoners, and demanded their release. The Marshal replied this was out of his power, but if he were determined to take them, he must get them the best way he could. Soon after Fries and his force arrived, Captain Jarrett came up, and the men saluted him with cheers. He had been to Philadelphia to surrender himself and be discharged on bail, and had just returned. He had an interview with the Marshal who requested him to get the men to withdraw. This he promised to do, but he either had no influence or did not choose to exercise it. He remained about there some two hours, but took no steps to quell the disturbance. After the interview with the Marshal, Fries returned to the guard and told his followers the result of it. Upon learning this they became quite violent and expressed a determination to have the prisoners at every risk. They abused Eyerley, the commissioner, and all who had assisted him, and towards them appeared to be more enraged than at the Marshal.

The insurgents now prepared to take the prisoners by force if they should not be given up peaceably. Fries told his men that four or five sentinels had to be passed, and begged them not to fire until the Marshal's posse had fired upon them; he would go on before them and expected to get the first blow. He cautioned them, a second time, not to fire first, and promised to give the word as soon as he was fired upon, when they must help themselves. He then gave the command, and his men followed toward the tavern. They came on with a rush and succeeded in getting into the entry in considerable numbers, where they were met by the Marshal's posse. A struggle took place between them, which resulted in the posse clearing the entry of the enemy. Esquire Horsfield came down stairs while the contest was going on, and, seeing that great excitement prevailed, he made his way through the crowd up stairs again to the landlord, Mr. Levering,¹ and prevailed upon him to close the bar, as liquor stimulated the disturbance. This repulse maddened the crowd, and they returned to the charge with greater fury than before, yelling and uttering savage shrieks. They struck the butts of their rifles on the ground, and fairly jumped with rage. They came to the door and a number entered and filled the hall. Those who remained outside pointed their rifles up at the windows to intimidate, and one, who entered, thrust the muzzle of his gun up the stairway, threatening to fire. They shouted their determination to have the prisoners. These proceedings caused great consternation among the Marshal's posse, who began to grow alarmed for their own safety.

Philip Schlaugh was so much frightened he mounted his horse when the second rush was made, and rode for Easton as fast as his animal could carry him. Esquire Horsfield begged the Marshal "for God's sake" to deliver up the prisoners, and worked his way down stairs to be ready to make his escape. The Marshal and his friends, up stairs at this time in charge of the prisoners, consulted with Judge Henry and others as to what was best to be done. He was advised to surrender the prisoners to Fries. This he refused to do, but said he would march them to Philadelphia, and if the mob thought proper to take them from him, on the way, it would be their act, not his, and he told them to prepare immediately to start for the city. Several refused to go, saying they would not thus endanger their lives, but if he would suffer them to return to their homes they would meet him in Philadelphia on Monday or Tuesday following. Fries was still demanding their release and threats of bodily harm were made against Eyerley, Henry and others, in case the prisoners were not given up. The Marshal, considering the lives of these gentlemen in

---

¹ Abraham Levering was the landlord of the Sun tavern at the time of the rescue of the prisoners, and the fifth in succession. He was a son of John and Susan Levering, Nazareth, and born December, 1757. His wife, Christiana, a daughter of Lewis Cassler, Lititz, was the popular hostess of the tavern for nine years. Levering entered upon the management June 1st, 1790; retired from the tavern in June, 1799, and died in Bethlehem, 1835.

danger, rather than expose them to injury, concluded to deliver the prisoners to Fries, and they were released and turned over to him. In a few minutes there was not an armed man on the ground, while the people of the town and neighborhood, who had collected as witnesses of the proceedings, quietly dispersed and returned to their homes. The contest was bloodless and the insurgents won.

# The Fries Rebellion.

## CHAPTER VII.

### The President Issues His Proclamation.

Immediately, after the rescue of the prisoners at Bethlehem, John Fries returned to his home in Milford township, but far from satisfied with the part he had taken in the affair. The excitement having subsided and reflection assumed its wonted sway, he doubted the propriety of his course, and began to have fears that he and his friends had gone beyond legal resistance. Like every man, who places himself in the wrong, he was anxious to unburden his mind by talking with others upon the subject, in the hope of justifying his conduct. For this purpose he went to see John Jamison,[1] an old acquaintance, two days after the occurrence, to whom he gave a full account of the affair at Bethlehem, and the part he took in it. He threw the blame upon the Germans, who, he said, he could do nothing with, as they had gotten the idea into their heads General Washington was opposed to the law, and therefore they need not allow it to be carried into execution.

An effort was now made to harmonize matters so the asssessments could be taken, thus putting an end to the disturbance that had so long agitated this and neighboring counties. It was agreed among the leading men in the disaffected districts of Bucks the proper course would be to meet and choose a committee from the three counties. For this purpose a meeting was called at the tavern of Conrad Marks, Monday, March 15, which some 200 people attended from the three counties. A committee of four from each county was appointed, with authority to consider the situation, and report what was best to be done under the circumstances. We have not been able

---

[1] John Jamison was a descendant of William Jamison, who settled in Richland township, in the neighborhood of Quakertown about 1730. He was a farmer and of no particular prominence.

to procure the names of all on the committee, but have several from this county; John Jamison, George Kline,[2] Daniel Roberts,[3] Conrad Marks, Dr. Baker, a man named Davis and Captain Jarrett. They advised the people to desist from further opposition to the assessors and other officers in the execution of their duties, and enjoined upon them to give due submission to the laws of their country. This seemed to be the sentiment of all present at the meeting, and no dissent was experienced. The people of Lower Milford were now in favor of having the assessments made, but, Mr. Roberts, upon being consulted, was not willing they should choose an assessor, but if Mr. Clark, who had not yet given up his commission, would take the rates, it would answer every purpose. A second meeting was advertised to be held at George Mitchel's tavern on March 25, to take the sense of the people upon the subject of permitting Clark to make the assessments. Fries was at the meeting held at Conrad Marks, and, as it does not appear he took any part in the proceedings, he probably quietly acquiesced with others in the peaceable measures adopted. Upon this occasion he and Mitchel had some conversation on the subject, when he admitted his former resistance to the law, a fact he never denied. He now expressed a willingness to give in his submission, and allow the law to be inforced. Apparently wishing to make some amends for his former harsh treatment of the officers, he told Jacob Huber that his house should not be assessed until he had given the assessors a dinner, and that if he were not at home when they came his son would be there to provide for them. With this the opposition to the law in Milford ended, and, from that time forward to his arrest, there was no better ordered citizen in the county than John Fries. He returned to his usual occupa-

---

[2] The Kline family were sympathizers with Fries in his opposition to the house tax law, and Jacob Kline, Sr., and three others of the name were arrested for treason. Jacob Kline was present at the meeting at Mitchel's tavern and was then well disposed.

[3] Daniel Roberts was a descendant of Edward Roberts, who, with his wife, settled near Quakertown, 1716. She was a daughter of Everard and Elizabeth Bolton, who settled at Cheltenham, Montgomery county, 1682. The ancestry of the Boltons is traced back to the Lord of Bolton, the lineal representative of the Saxon Earls of Murcia. The late Judge Roberts, of Doylestown, was a descendant of Edward Roberts.

tion, vendue crying, and, if his present good conduct be any evidence, he had entirely repented his previous course.

The Marshal kept Judge Peters fully informed of the operations of the insurgents, and also of his own movements. Immediately upon the rescue of the prisoners at Bethlehem he announced the fact to the Judge, who laid the matter before the Federal authorities without delay. Upon being thus officially informed of the truth of what had heretofore reached him in the shape of rumors, although pretty well authenticated, the President called his cabinent together to deliberate upon the steps to be taken in relation thereto. They were now fully cognizant of the resistance that had been offered to the law, and was satisfied it could not be executed in the disaffected districts unless the opposition should end. It was now determined the President should issue his proclamation, and endeavor, by this mild means, to call the deluded disturbers of the peace back to their duty, before a resort was had to harsher measures. For this purpose he caused to be issued, from the seat of government at Philadelphia on March 12, 1799, the following:

*By the President of the United States of America :*

### PROCLAMATION.

WHEREAS, combinations, to defeat the execution of the laws for the valuation of lands and dwelling houses within the United States, have existed within the counties of Northampton, Montgomery and Bucks, in the State of Pennsylvania, have proceeded in a manner subversive of the just authority of the government, by misrepresentations to render the laws odious, by deterring the officers of the United States to forbear the execution of their functions, and by openly threatening their lives. And, whereas, the endeavors of the well-effected citizens, as well as of the executive officers to conciliate compliance with these laws, have failed of success, and certain persons in the county of Northampton, aforesaid, have been hardy enough to perpetrate certain acts, which, I am advised, amount to treason, being overt acts of levying war against the United States, the said persons exceeding one hundred in number, and armed and arrayed in warlike manner, having, on the seventh day of the present month of March, proceeded to the house of Abraham Levering, in the town of Bethlehem, and there compelled William Nichols, Marshal of the United States, for the District of Pennsylvania, to desist from the execution of certain legal processes in his hands to be executed, and having compelled him to discharge and set at liberty, certain persons whom he had arrested by virtue of a criminal process, duly issued for offenses against the United States, and having impeded and prevented the commissioners and assessor, in conformity with the laws aforesaid, in the county of Northampton, aforesaid, by threats of personal injury, from executing the said laws, avowing, as the motive of these illegal and treasonable proceedings, an intention to prevent, by force of arms, the execution of the said laws, and to withstand, by open violence, the lawful authority of the United States. And, whereas, by the Constitution and laws of the United States, I am authorized, whenever the laws of the United States shall be opposed, or the execution thereof obstructed in any State, by combinations too powerful to be suppressed by the ordinary course of judicial proceedings, or by powers, vested in the Marshal, to call forth military force to supress such combinations, and to cause the laws to be duly executed, and I have accordingly determined so to do, under the solemn conviction that the essential interests of the United States demand it.

*Therefore*, I, John Adams, President of the United States, do hereby command all persons, being insurgents as aforesaid, and all others whom it may concern, on or before Monday next, being the eighteenth day of the present month, to disperse and retire peaceably to their respective abodes: and I do, moreover, warn all persons whomsoever, against aiding, abetting or comforting the perpetrators of the aforesaid treasonable acts, and I do require all officers and others, good and faithful citizens, according to their respective duties and laws of the land, to exert their utmost endeavors to prevent and suppress, such dangerous and unlawful proceedings.

In testimony thereof, I have caused the Seal of the United

States of America to be affixed to these presents, and signed the same with my hand. Done at the city of Philadelphia, the twelfth day of March, in the year of our Lord, 1799, and of the Independence of the said United States of America, the twenty-third.

By the President:

(Signed)     JOHN ADAMS.
(Signed)     TIMOTHY PICKERING,
                               Secretary of State.

The proclamation reached Milford township, on the fifteenth of March. Its appearance created a good deal of excitement and talk among the people, who were now convinced the government was disposed to treat the late disturbance with more seriousness than the participators in it had believed. It was reported to the meeting at Conrad Marks, on the eighteenth, where it became the subject of discussion and conversation. On the evening of the day, it first made its appearance in the township, George Mitchel carried a copy down to Frederick Heaney's, to whom he read it, who agreed to submit to it; and he made no further opposition. Soon after the appearance of the proclamation, a statement of the part John Fries had taken in opposing the law was published in the newspapers; Israel Roberts carried a copy to him to read what was said of him. The account of his conduct, as published, seemed to affect him greatly; and, upon being questioned, he admitted he had never before considered the matter in such serious light as he had within a few days. He said he had not slept half an hour for three or four nights, and that he would give all he was worth in the world if the matter were settled and he clear of it. He expressed a willingness to surrender himself if the government would send for him.

The meeting advertised at George Mitchel's tavern, on March twenty-five, was held at that time. About forty persons were present, among them, John Fries and Frederick Heaney. It was agreed that Clark should make the assements. Neither Fries nor Heaney voted upon the question, but both expressed a willingness that others should do so, and, in fact, hoped they might vote for him. They seemed to yield entire obedience to the authorities, and appeared sensible of their previous misconduct. In Northampton county, the reception of the President's proclamation had the same good effect as in Bucks, and almost wholly quieted the disturbance. But little opposition to the law took place after that date, the most serious being the attack on Mr. Balliott, a collector. He was waylaid upon his return from Bethlehem, whether he had been on business, and so severely beaten a physician was brought from that place to attend him. His injuries, however, proved not to be very serious, and he soon recovered. About the same time Henry Artman, Adam Stephen and Henry Shankwyler, of Millarstown, went to Philadelphia, and surrendered themselves to the Federal authorities, and entered into bail before Judge Peters for their appearance. These men were among the most violent opposers of the law in Northampton county. The opposition to the law had the effect of causing a repeal of the provisions of the house tax, requiring a statement of the windows of each dwelling, at the sessions of 1798-99, and before the most serious disturbances had taken place.

The reader, no doubt, will be as much astonished as the writer, at the course of the government after this period. From and after March 25 John Fries and his aiders and abettors gave their entire submission to the authorities, and comported themselves as quietly and orderly as the best citizens. They allowed their property to be assessed, and acquiesced in the law being carried into execution. Under all the circumstances it does not appear that the extreme measures afterwards pursued were called for, but that a lenient government, such as ours professes to be, should have overlooked the faults and even offenses of the past, in consideration that a very obnoxious law, and at best of questionable propriety, was allowed to go into full force and effect. The pursuing of Fries, in this view of the case, had the appearance of persecution, which created greater sympathy, in his behalf, than would otherwise have been extended to him.

The President's proclamation gave the proceedings of the insurgents, in Bucks and Northampton, an importance they otherwise would not have received; and, from this time forward to the conclusion of the "Rebellion," it was a National affair, and attracted the attention of all sections of the Union. Many expected to see another "Western Insurrection" or a "Shay's Rebellion," with a more disastrous termination. The timid friends of republican government were alarmed lest this disturbance might be a rock on which the ship of State would founder and go to pieces, while the enemies of our institutions predicted such would be the result, and appeared delighted at the prospective overthrow of the government.

The President caused his proclamation to be immediately sent to the Governor of Pennsylvania, then in Philadelphia attending upon the session of the Legislature, and Governor Mifflin[1] transmitted a copy to the Assembly, accompanied by the following message:

*Message of the Governor of Pennsylvania, to the Two Houses of Assembly:*

GENTLEMEN:—It is announced, by proclamation issued by the President of the United States, dated the 12th inst., that combinations, to defeat the execution of the laws for the valuation of lands and dwelling houses within the United States, have existed in the counties of Northampton, Montgomery and Bucks, in the State of Pennsylvania: That in the judgment of the President it is necessary to call for the military force, in order to suppress the combinations aforesaid, and cause the laws aforesaid to be duly executed; and that the President has accordingly determined to do so, under the

---

[1] Thomas Mifflin was born in Philadelphia, 1744, of Quaker parentage, and brought up to mercantile pursuits. When the war for independence broke out, Congress appointed and commissioned him a Brigadier-General and he was given command of the Pennsylvania troops. He served with great credit in various positions, among which was Quartermaster-General. He was elected a member of Congress, 1783, and made Speaker. In this capacity he acted during the closing scenes of the Revolution and received back the commission of Washington when he formally tendered his resignation. He was elected Governor of Pennsylvania, 1790, the first under the new Constitution, and served three terms, nine years. He died at Lancaster, January 21, 1800.

solemn conviction that the essential interest of the United States demands it.

That I have received no communication from the President on this important occasion, yet it is my duty, as Executive Magistrate of Pennsylvania, to call your attention to the subject, that if any means ought to be taken on the part of the State to co-operate with the Federal government, they may be devised and authorized by the Legislature.

(Signed) THOMAS MIFFLIN.

*Philadelphia, March 14, 1799.*

The matter was referred to a committee of the House, which made report condemning the disturbance in the strongest terms, but proceeded to say, that as the President had taken proper steps to quell the insurrection, they did not deem it necessary for the State to take any action in the matter; but whenever it should become necessary to co-operate with the general government they would do so cheerfully. To the report was addeded the following resolution, but was stricken out on its passage:

*Resolved,* " That the Governor be, and is hereby requested to cause full and due inquiry into the causes of the said riots, to be made, and to make special report to this House thereupon, and particularly of any circumstances which may be alleged, or discovered, tending to show the origin of the same agency of foreign incendiaries, in the seditions views of domestic traitors."

# The Fries Rebellion.

## CHAPTER VIII.

Troops Called Out to Suppress the Insurrection.

While the Legislature took no further action concerning the house tax troubles, the Representatives from Northampton county issued an address to the people of the State, in which they say that, on a recent visit to their constituency, they found nothing that "looks like an insurrection." They were highly indignant at the course of the Federal government, as were the people of the State, generally. There was now a change of policy; the "Fries Rebellion" was relegated to the military arm for treatment.

On March 20 the Secretary of War made the following requisition, on Governor Mifflin, for militia to assist in quelling the insurrection :

WAR DEPARTMENT, March 20, 1799.

*Sir :*—To suppress the insurrection now existing in the counties of Northampton, Bucks and Montgomery, in the State of Pennsylvania, in opposition to the laws of the United States, the President has thought it best to employ a military force, to be composed, in part, of such of the militia of Pennsylvania whose situation and state of preparation will enable them to march with promptitude. As the corps of militia first desired on this occasion are the troops of cavalry belonging to this city, and one troop from each of the counties of Philadelphia, Bucks, Chester, Montgomery and Lancaster, these troops I have the honor to request your Excellency will order to hold themselves in readiness to march, on, or before, the 28th instant, under the command of Brigadier-General Macpherson.[1]

I have the honor to be, with the greatest respect, your Excellency's most obedient servant.

(Signed) JAMES MCHENRY.[2]

His Excellency, THOMAS MIFFLIN.

Upon the receipt of the Secretary of War's communication, Governor Mifflin addressed the following letter to the Adjutant-General of the State, directing him to issue general orders for complying with the President's request:

"PHILADELPHIA, March 20, 1799, 3 o'clock, p. m."

"*Sir:*—The Secretary of War, has this moment communicated to me, the President's intention to employ a military force, in suppressing the insurrection now existing in the counties of Northampton, Bucks and Montgomery, with a request that the Troops of Cavalry, belonging to this city, and a troop from each of the counties of Philadelphia, Bucks, Chester, Montgomery and Lancaster, may be ordered to hold themselves in readiness to march on, or before, the 28th instant, under the command of Brigadier-General Macpherson.

"You will, therefore, issue general orders for complying with the President's request; and communicate by express with the commanding officers of the several corps. As soon as the troops are ready to march you will make your report to me, sending the returns of the officers from time to time as you receive them." I am, sir,

Your most obedient Servant,

(Signed) THOMAS MIFFLIN.

To PETER BAYNTON,[3] ESQ.,

Adjutant General of Militia of Pennsylvania.

---

[1] William Macpherson, the son of Captain John Macpherson, Philadelphia, was an officer in the 16th British foot. At the first opportunity he sold out his commission and succeeded in escaping from the British lines to Philadelphia, where he offered his services to the Board of War. He was commissioned a major in the Pennsylvania line. His brother John, a Captain, fell at Quebec.

[2] James McHenry, Secretary of War, from 1796 to 1800, was born in Maryland, 1753, and died in Baltimore, May 8, 1819. He served in the Revolution as aide-de-camp of Lafayette; was a delegate from Maryland to the Continental Congress, 1783-86; a member of the Convention that formed the Federal Constitution, 1787, and appointed Secretary of War by Mr. Adams.

[3] The records show that Peter Baynton was appointed Adjutant-General of Pennsylvania, February 27, 1799, and vacated the office May 1, 1800. We have not been able to find any further mention of him.

## THE FRIES REBELLION. 77

In obedience to the order of his immediate Commander-in-Chief, Adjutant-General Baynton issued orders calling into service a portion of the militia of the State, as follows:

"GENERAL ORDERS."

"PHILADELPHIA, March 20, 1799."
"The following corps of cavalry are to hold themselves in readiness to march on, or before, the 28th instant:

"Captain Dunlap's, Captain Singer's, Captain Morrell's, Captain Leeper's, of the city of Philadelphia; Captain Lesher's, of the county of Philadelphia; Captain Sims',[4] of the county of Bucks; Captain Taylor's, of the county of Chester; Captain Montgomery's, of the county of Lancaster, and Captain Kennedy's, of the county of Montgomery.

"Officers commanding the above troops of Cavalry will make report to the Adjutant-General as soon as their respective corps are ready to march."
"By order of the Commander-in-Chief."
(Signed) "PETER BAYNTON,"
"Adjutant-General of the Militia of Pennsylvania."

Of the quota of troops called for, one company of cavalry was taken from Bucks and another from Montgomery, but Northampton was so far gone in rebellion her militia were not thought reliable, and none were taken from that county. The President designated William Macpherson as commander of the troops about to make the expedition into Bucks and Northampton, and, to give him sufficient rank, he was ap-

---

[4] Walter Sims bought the China Retreat property, 361 acres, 1798. This was a famous place in its day, on the west bank of the Delaware three miles below Bristol. In 1787 the farm belonged to one Benger, an Irish sporting gentleman, who imported the famous horse Messenger. He sold it to one Van Braam Houchgust, the Dutch Governor of an East India island, who erected an elegant mansion upon it, and named it "China Retreat." From him it passed to Captain Sims. Captain John Green, son-in-law of Captain Sims, was the first American sea captain to carry our flag to China. He died, in 1797. In 1833 an additional building was erected and a school established there called "Bristol College," but lived only a few years. The buildings were used as an hospital during the War of the Rebellion, and afterward a State school for the education of colored soldiers' orphans, was opened there. Captain Alden Partridge established a military school at China Retreat about 1842-3, which was kep up for a few years.

pointed a Brigadier-General in the United States army on
March 18. At the time he held the same commission in the
militia of Pennsylvania, which he resigned on the 22d, so as
to accept the new honors that awaited him.  General Macpherson resided in Philadelphia, and, after the Revolution
raised and commanded a celebrated volunteer corps known as
the "Macpherson Blues," which, in its day, was the best
drilled corps of citizen soldiery in the country.  The troop of
cavalry ordered out from Bucks belonged to the lower end of
the county, and commanded by Captain Walter Sims. He
was preparing to leave the country when the order of the
Adjutant-General was issued, and, the next day, tendered his
resignation as captain. The letter was addressed to the first
lieutenant, William Rodman,⁵ and answered on the 23d, in the
name of the company. As we have not found any evidence of
an election to fill the vacancy of Captain Sims being held before the troop marched, it probably went out under Lieutenant
Rodman. General Macpherson subsequently ordered out a
company of cavalry from Cumberland county.

Not considering the militia called out sufficient to quell the
disturbance, the War Department ordered all the regulars
that could be spared from other service to join them. The
number was about 500, and they were ordered to rendezvous
at Newtown⁶ and Bristol⁷ and from there proceed to the seat
of war. Two companies left New York, March 17, for Bristol, there to await the arrival of other troops; a detachment,

---

⁵ William Rodman, grandson of Dr. John Rodman, who settled at Burlington, N. J.,
early in the last century, was born in Bensalem township, Bucks county, 1757. He was a
patriot in the Revolution; a member of the State Senate, and was elected to Congress
in 1812, serving two terms. The late Mrs. John Fox, of Doylestown, was his niece,
daughter of his Brother Gilbert.

⁶ Newtown, the county seat of Bucks county from 1725 to 1813, is situated in a delight-
ful country, six miles from the Delaware and twenty-five from Philadelphia. The population is about 1500. It was to this place Washington brought the captured Hessians
from Trenton, December 26, 1776.

⁷ Bristol is on the west bank of the Delaware, opposite Burlington, N. J., twenty
miles above Philadelphia. It was made the county seat of Bucks in 1705, and so remained until its removal to Newtown in 1725. It is the only sea-port in the county.
Population, 5000.

under Captain John Henry⁸ reached Trenton⁹ from New York on the 23d; encamped there over night, and marched to Newtown the next morning, there to await further orders. On the 21st a detachment of artillery, under Lieutenant Woolstencroft[10] passed through Harrisburg from Reading: on the 27th Captain Irvine's[11] artillery marched from Carlisle;[12] and, on the 30th, a company, commanded by Captain Shoemaker,[13] sixty strong, passed through Lancaster[14], all for the

---

[8] John Henry, Pennsylvania, was appointed captain of artilleryists and engineers June 1, 1798, and resigned December 31, 1801.

[9] Trenton, the capital of New Jersey, is at the head of tide water on the Delaware. It was founded by William Trent, a successful merchant of Philadelphia, about 1715. Trent died in 1724. The town increased rapidly. It was made a borough in 1746, and a post office established as early as 1734. This was the scene of the capture of the Hessians by Washington, the turning of the tide in Revolutionary affairs. The population of Trenton is about 75,000 and it is the seat of extensive and valuable manufactures.

[10] Charles Woolstencroft, of Pennsylvania, was appointed lieutenant 2d artillerists and engineers June 4, 1798; in regiment of artillerists April 1, 1802; promoted captain March 15, 1805; transferred to corps of artillery May 12, 1814, and died September 28, 1817. He received the brevet rank of major March 15, 1815, for 10 years' faithful service in one grade.

[11] Callender Irvine, of Pennsylvania, was appointed captain 2d artillerists and engineers June 1, 1798, and resigned May 20, 1801; appointed superintendent of military stores October 24, 1804; appointed commissary general of purchases August 8, 1812, and died October 9, 1841, at Philadelphia, Penna.

[12] Carlisle, the county seat of Cumberland, was laid out in 1701, and a survey of the town and adjacent lands made in 1702. It was so named from Carlisle, in Cumberland county, England. In 1753 it contained but five dwellings. It was the seat of a government cavalry school for many years; the barracks being built in 1777 by the Hessians captured at Trenton were burnt down by Lees forces when they invaded the Cumberland Valley in June, 1863. Dickinson's College, chartered by the Legislature, 1783, is located at Carlisle. Few sections of the State are richer in historic incidents.

[13] Peter Shoemaker, of Pennsylvania, was appointed ensign, 2d infantry, April 11, 1792; in 2d sub-legion, September 4, 1792; 1st lieutenant, March 3, 1793; captain, March 3, 1799; honorably discharged June 29, 1800.

[14] The city of Lancaster, the capital of the county of the same name, is on the Pennsylvania railroad, between Philadelphia and Harrisburg, sixty miles from the latter. It was laid out by Governor Hamilton, 1730; became the seat of justice in 1734, and was incorporated, 1742. It was an important place in Revolutionary times. Congress repaired there in September, 1777, and thence removed to York. It is the seat of Franklin and Marshal College. Lancaster is in the heart of one of the very finest agricultural regions in the country, and for a long time enjoyed the reputation of being the largest inland town in the United States. It contains many industries. Lancaster was the capital of the State for some time, and the seat of government was removed to Harrisburg, 1812.

same destination. The President also made requisition on the executive of New Jersey for two thousand militia, to hold themselves in readiness to march. Of this force the eight troops of cavalry were to be prepared to march at a moment's notice. The order provides that, "Those who shall be warned for duty in consequence of these orders are to take care that their swords be not loose, but well riveted in their belts, that their blades be sharp and bright, their pistols clean, and in good order for videt duty; their horses at all times well shod, fed, and gently exercised, their saddles and valise pads well stuffed, and their girths and breast plates sufficiently strong." This order was issued on March 22. As Governor Mifflin was an old soldier he understood the importance of minute directions on such occasion. At a meeting of Captain Mosher s company of infantry, at Lancaster, it was resolved they were ready to march at a moment's warning for the support of government. The *Daily Advertiser*, of March 30, says that various detachments of regular troops are already on the march for Northampton, which will, it is supposed, form a body of about 500 men.

The time for the marching of the force from Philadelphia under the immediate command of General Macpherson, was fixed for April 3, and on the first instant the following orders were issued:

"GENERAL ORDERS."

The troops, which are under orders to march on Wednesday, the 3d instant, will assemble on their own parades precisely at 8 o'clock, a. m., on that day, in a complete state of preparation to take up the line of march.

"The different commanding officers will receive their instructions as to the route, &c., on Tuesday morning at 10 o'clock, for which purpose they will attend at my quarters. Lieutenant John Williams, of the 2d troop of cavalry, of the Blues, is appointed aide-de-camp, and is to be respected accordingly."       (Signed)     WILLIAM MACPHERSON,
*Philadelphia, April 1, 1799.*                    Brigadier-General.

For some reason, not explained, the march of the troops was delayed until Thursday, April 4, at 8 o'clock, a. m., to which effect orders were issued on the 2d. The command was to rendezvous on the evening of that day at the Spring House tavern, on the Ridge Road, sixteen miles from Philadelphia, whence they were to march for the disaffected districts.

Despite the orders to march on the 4th, the entire force did not leave on that day. One company of United States Artillery, commanded by Captain Elliott,[15] left the city on the 3d, the day first named, and, on Friday, the 5th, two troops of volunteer cavalry, and the four city troops of horse, got off, but the main body, under command of General Macpherson in person, left the morning of the 4th. They assembled at their quarters at an early hour; thence proceeded to the place of general rendezvous, and took up the march amid the shouts of the populace. As they passed through the city to the sounds of martial music, with flying colors, and "decked in all the pomp, pride and circumstance of glorious war," they created a great sensation. The streets were lined with citizens who had turned out to witness the display; and while the men whirled their hats and shouted their huzzas, the ladies waved their handkerchiefs and otherwise manifested their admiration of the glittering pageant. But once since the close of the war of Independence had so large a body of troops been called together in this section of the Union, and, upon this occasion, the number, as well as the nature of their service, caused the display to receive more than usual eclat. Passing out of the city the troops struck the Ridge Road,[16] along which they marched to the Spring House, Montgomery county, where they made their camp the same evening.

As they marched through the country, the people flocked to

---

[15] Joseph Elliott, South Carolina, was appointed Lieutenant of Artillery, March 14, 1792; transferred to 1st artillery and engineers, May 9, 1794; promoted captain July 19, 1796, and resigned December 29, 1800.

[16] The Ridge Road opened about 1700-1701, was one of the early roads leading from the Whitemarsh district to Philadelphia. In "Watson's Annals" I find this mention of it: "William Harmer, John Fisher, Daniel Howell, Edward Burch, Thomas Rutter and Nicholas Scull applied (to Colonial Council) for a road from the limekilns for carting of lime to Philadelphia, extending from the 'kilns into Plymouth road near Bressoon.' This was the beginning of this road. The recent History of Montgomery county says: "We

the highways to gaze at the "Federal Army," as they called it, but, as the expedition was disapproved, they received but few marks of approbation in the rural districts.

Headquarters was still at the Spring House on the 9th, on which day General Macpherson issued an address to the inhabitants of the disaffected districts. It was published in German, and the object appears to have been to call the people back to their duty; but inasmuch as they had ceased their opposition to the law some time before, and quietly submited to its provisions, the address was uncalled for and without effect. The advent of the troops had a tendency to irritate any existing soreness in the public mind, instead of allaying it, and therefore did harm instead of good. The following is the address:

"William Macpherson, Brigadier-General" of the armies of the United States, commander of the troops ordered to act against the insurgents of the counties of Northampton, Montgomery and Bucks, in the State of Pennsylvania, to the people of the aforesaid counties:

FELLOW CITIZENS:—" Being ordered by the President of the United States to employ the troops under my command, or, according to circumstances, further military force to procure submission to the laws of the United States, and to suppress and disperse all unlawful combinations, which have been made to obstruct the execution of the aforesaid laws, or any of them, by main force and power, I, therefore, have thought

---

know, by William Scull's map, of 1770, that the Egypt or Ridge road had been laid out for several years, for it is denoted thereon as leading to Friends' Meeting house in Providence." On a map of Norriton, made in 1771, it is called "Road to Philadelphia called Egypt road." It was extended through the borough of Norristown sometime before 1770. The Ridge Road terminates in Philadelphia at Ninth and Vine streets, and is known after it enters the city limits as Ridge Avenue, and is a much traveled highway leading to the northwestern part of the city, on which a line of passenger cars runs. In 1829, the United States mail was robbed on the Ridge Road, within the present built-up portion of the city, which created great excitement at the time. The robbers, Porter, Wilson and Potete were arrested and tried. One of them turned states evidence and the two others were hanged. How far General Macpherson marched on the Ridge Road before leaving it and striking across country to the Bethlehem road along which he marched to reach the Spring House, is not known. No doubt he marched up Ninth street, to Vine, and there took the Ridge Road, as this seems to have been his most practicable way of leaving the city.

it proper to inform the people of the said counties, and all others whom it may concern, of the danger to which they expose themselves by combining in unlawful proceedings, or giving any assistance or encouragement to those who are concerned therein; and likewise to represent to them how just it is to submit to the laws, in general, but particularly to those against which they have opposed themselves in the most violent manner. It cannot be unknown to you, my fellow citizens, nor to any part of the people of the United States that submission to the laws, constitutionally made, is absolutely necessary for the support of the government; and that in a republic, where laws are made by general consent, this consent must be manifested by the majority of such persons as have been appointed for that purpose by the people in general, according to the constitution."

After pointing out the duty and necessity of the people to submit to the laws when made, he proceeds to discuss the constitutional power of Congress to lay the tax in question, and points out the article under which the law was passed. " The United States were threatened with the resentment of a very powerful, very ambitious and very revengeful nation," and that the tax was necessary to raise money in order "to provide for the common defense and general welfare" of the country. He next speaks of the tax and the manner in which it was to be assessed, of which he says:

" In laying this tax Congress paid the greatest attention to the situation and wants of the people, and distributed it in such manner the burden almost totally falls on the richer part, and the poorer class are greatly screened from the effects thereof. It is laid on land, dwelling houses and slaves; but as there are no slaves in this State, the whole tax falls upon the lands and dwelling houses. The lands are to be taxed exactly to their value, be the owner whom he may, but the dwelling houses are appraised at a different rate. The poor man whose house, outhouses and lot, not exceeding two acres, are worth less than $100 has nothing to pay; and if it were worth $100 the tax would be only 20 cents. According to the same rule, other houses of a higher value pay as follows: If worth $200, 40 cents; $300, 60 cents; $400, 80 cents, and $500, one dollar, from which you will perceive, my fellow citizens, that the house tax is according to the value of the house, at 20 cents to $100: but for houses from $500 to a $1000 value the tax rises for each $100, 30 cents; so that a house of the value of $600 will have to pay six times 30 cents or $1.80. If worth $700, $2.10; $800, $2.40; $900, $2.70; $1000, $3.

"At this rate the rich man, with a house rated at $1000, has to pay three times as much tax as the poor man whose house is rated at one-half that sum, viz: $500; and thus the tax operates progressively to the most costly houses and opulent people, until the value of their houses is taxed in proportion, five times as high as those of their poorer fellow citizens, whose houses are worth only from $100 to $500. A house worth $100 pays 20 cents, which is only the one-fifth part of one per cent. of its value; a house worth $30,000 pays $300, which is one whole per cent. of its value, and consequently five times as much in proportion as the former. Hereby, my fellow citizens, you must be convinced that an opposition to this tax in our counties is not only contrary to the Constitution, the laws, and every principle of good government, but, in itself, inconsistent and ridiculous, as the tax which is opposed is the most easy on the poorest citizens, whom they irritate to opposition. Many of their houses, however, would have no tax to pay, and very few more than $1.00 each, for very few of their houses would be rated at more than $500. It is true, they will be subject to a land tax, but the tax on houses must first be deducted from the whole quota of the State, and what is then deficient will be laid upon the land. The houses in this State will probably pay the greatest part of the tax, perhaps the whole, and, in that case, no tax will be laid upon the land, and those whose houses are rated at less than one hundred dollars will be exempt from the tax. As a further proof of the attention of Congress to the wishes and accommodations of the people, they have, during the last session, repealed that part which required a statement of the windows of each dwelling house, and which, as it afterward appeared, was more disagreeable than necessary or useful. Therefore no further account of the windows has been demanded. To ascertain the value of the lands and houses was a difficult matter, and connected with a great deal of expense, but when once done need not be repeated. Great pains were taken and the most effective measures employed to select people of good character who understood the business well, and whose interest were equally involved with their fellow citizens to have the business accurately executed. "Besides, this act is not perpetual, being only for one year, and will not be continued unless the public good demands it, and not otherwise than with the consent of the people through their representatives. As for those who have, in so treasonable a manner, opposed the execution of such lawful, necessary, and, for that part of the citizens who are the least able to pay taxes, indulgent law, there can, therefore, be no excuse. The bad consequences which they draw upon themselves by their criminal conduct they cannot impute but to their own blindness, obstinacy and malice. On the contrary, every necessary step will, and must be, taken to bring them, and all others who have aided and abetted them, to submission and trial by due course of law, in order that their punishment may serve as an example to others and prevent a like course in the future. The necessity of employing arms against a number of our fellow citizens is painful, but the consequences must be imputed to those, whose traitorous conduct has produced the present disturbances, and not to government, who, according to its most sacred duties, is obliged to maintain order, and enforce obedience to the laws.

"But all those who return quietly to their homes, and abstain from any participation in these unlawful acts, either through open aid or secret abetting, counsel, or information, shall obtain the utmost protection to their persons and property.

"Every precaution shall be taken that the march of the troops shall not be troublesome to the citizens; all subsistance shall be punctually paid for, and the strictest discipline observed. Let me, therefore, my fellow citizens, warn and entreat you as you love your country and extenuate the happiness consistent with liberty, order and peace; as you wish to avoid the necessity of human bloodshed, which is as much repugnant to my wishes as those of the President; as you abhor the horrors of a civil war, and the crimes and punishment of traitors, let me conjure you to shut your ears against the counsels of those malicious persons who would lead you to destruction in order to satisfy their own ambition, while they screen themselves from punishment due to their crimes; who try to seduce you to take up arms against the laws and governments of your country, and involve yourselves in a contest, as hopeless as it is criminal, against the power of the United States; who speak to you of peace and liberty while they are kindling civil war; who complain of expenses while they are forcing the government to augment them, in order to suppress sedition and revolt; and who plume themselves upon being Republicans, while transgressing the most essential principles of Republican government; to wit: obedience to the laws made by the decision of the majority.

"Therefore, I forewarn you not to aid or abet those violaters of the law in any manner, so that you may avoid a participation of their crimes, and the consequent punishment.

"Given under my hand and seal at Headquarters, April 6, 1799."

    (Signed)  WILLIAM MACPHERSON.
    (Signed)  JOHN WILLIAMS, Aid-de-Camp.

# The Fries Rebellion.

## CHAPTER IX.

### Rev. Charles Henry Helmuth Issues an Address

When the address of General Macpherson was published, it was accompanied by a letter, from the Rev. Mr. Helmuth,[1] addressed to the German population in general, and the people of Northampton, in particular:

"TO THE PEOPLE OF NORTHAMPTON COUNTY."

"*Friends and Brethren in the Faith* :—Excuse my addressing these lines to you ; where there is fire, everybody is bound to extinguish it, and the clergyman is no more to be blamed for lending his aid than any other citizen. I am depressed with anxiety on your account. I know the consequence of conduct like yours ; many of you will doubtless be apprehended and confined, some perhaps will pay the forfeit with their lives. You know it is the duty of the clergy of the city to warn such miserable persons, and prepare them as much as in their power for the awful change. My heart was much oppressed.

---

[1] J. Henry Charles Helmuth was a distinguished Lutheran clergyman, of Philadelphia, for his piety and zeal, and he is credited with hoping his appeal to the German population might restore quiet and order. We give both the address of General Macpherson and Mr. Helmuth because they are part of the documents bearing on the "Rebellion," and help to make up its history. Macpherson's address is a stilted affair and not called for. From its date, the Rev. Helmuth's letter was written before the troops marched, and not published until after that of the General's. A citizen of Northampton replied to it with some bitterness, calling him to account for meddling with things that did not concern him. We were not able to find a copy of this letter among the contemporaneous records and newspapers we examined.

"I thought, alas! perhaps the same circumstances as those of 1794 will again occur; perhaps other thoughtless people will fall into the same wretched situation because they were ignorant, and were deluded, and what would be your feelings if you had to witness their sorrow and anguish, their agonies of death? You should have warned the miserable creatures; he would then perhaps have been saved; but you neglected to warn him, and are therefore responsible for the destruction of him and his. Such were the melancholy reflections that induced me to write you these lines.

"I trust that you will think, when you read this, as you may in truth: This man is sincere for our welfare—why then should we think it improper in him to send us this advice? If he even should now and then say some things that are not perfectly agreeable to us we will still take it in good part, for, perhaps, he is in the right, perhaps we have been deluded, we may have been deceived. If such be your thoughts you will soon find them perfectly correct.

"You have hitherto entitled yourselves to the character of industrious and religious citizens of the Union, and most of the Germans still deserve that praise; but, sorrowful to relate, you have suffered yourselves to be spurred on to the most abominable injustice, to actual rebellion against the government you yourselves have chosen. How happy it is that your number is but small, amongst the serious, and that the far greater part of them view your inconsiderate conduct with detestation! You all know that government cannot exist without taxes; at least your Bible should so instruct you; read Romans, 12th chap., 1-7; read it attentively.

"Do but reflect reasonably on your conduct. Even the holy passion week have you profaned with the works of actual rebellion. You have undertaken to oppose a tax, which is as favorable to the country people as any tax can possibly be; for the rich inhabitants of the cities pay by far the greatest proportion of it; you have undertaken to oppose the tax which never would have been made had not the government been necessitated to make defensive preparations against the attacks of the French; a nation that aims at the overthrow and destruction of all religion, against a people that would scarcely have dared to attack and plunder us if they had not been certain they had their advocates among us.

"You do not consider the dreadful consequences of such opposition as you have made; I will therefore inform you of some of them.

"In the first place, an army of several thousand men will be marched into your neighborhood; you well know that in spite of every possible attention of commanding officers, excesses will be committed by an army. You will be more or less prevented from following your usual occupations, and yourselves and families will be put in greater terror and apprehension.

"Second, The army will cost money, and the money the government will have to raise by direct taxes, for which you must thank your own opposition. The western expedition in 1794 cost a million of dollars; from this you may judge what expenses you will bring on yourselves and fellow citizens by your scandalous insurrections.

"Thirdly, If you make any further opposition you will necessarily be treated as rebels, and, before a month has passed, many of you will be in prison. They will be torn from their wives and children, and some will probably suffer an ignominious death.

"Alas! my heart bleeds for you. You have been told a thousand falsehoods. You have been told that the militia approved of your violence, and would not march against you. But you have been wrongfully deceived. For my own part I have heard many speak of your conduct, but I have not heard one approve of it; your best friends (if those are your best friends who agreed with you in political opinions) say the occurrences in Northampton are very unjustifiable; the insurgents must be subdued; what would become of us if everybody were to create an insurrection? This is the substance of what is thought and said of your conduct—and you may depend upon it, that the government could, at a very short notice, muster upward of 20,000 men, if such a number were necessary, who would willingly march against you. Every one cries shame! shame! upon you.

"I beseech you to mark well the character of these men who have enticed you to this insurrection. Are there not many of them who spend more money at the taverns in the course of a few evenings than their whole tax amounts to? Honest Christian men will never advise to rebellion, but more especially against a government which has scarcely its equal under the sun. No; they are wicked, restless men, who have deceived themselves and you.

"It is your misfortune that you have suffered the habit, to grow upon you, of scandalizing the government; of cursing, instead of blessing it; and then indeed there are enough to be found, who, having particular ends in view, will scheme with you; persons who wish for your friendship on election day, in order that they may get a lucrative office under the very government that they blaspheme. When matters come to extremities, these deluders know perfectly well how to slip their necks out of the halter and let the deluded suffer. These, who, in comparison with the former, are innocent, will be left to bake as their deceivers have brewed. Think of me when you experience this sorrowful truth.

"Alas! you have been most scandalously deceived: from my soul I pity you! But what is now to be done? Listen, and take my advice. It is possible that the Marshal will be sent with an armed force to seize the wretches who opposed him in arms. For God's sake do not let yourselves be prevailed upon to abet those rebels; for should you be found in their company, you will certainly be punished with them.

"Rather endeavor to persuade them to deliver themselves up to the proper authority, and this would be the wisest course they could pursue; but if they will not do so give the Marshal every assistance he may require, for it is your duty.

"Take my advice; affection for you and the impulse of conscience have compelled me to write you this letter.

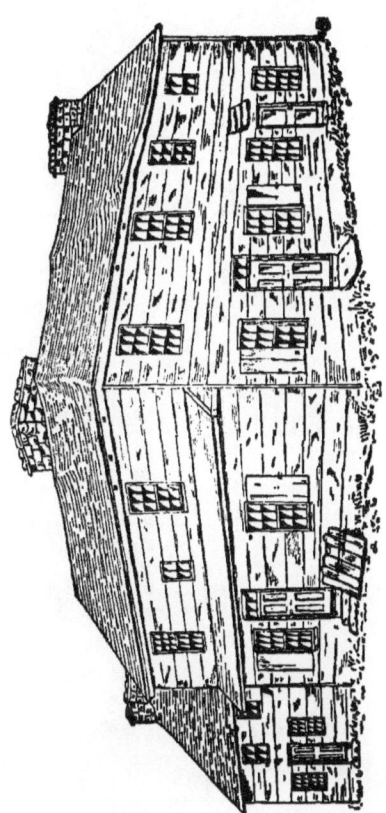

If you follow my counsels you will do well, if not, I have done my duty. Be assured that I remain your friend,"
(Signed) "J. HENRY CHARLES HELMUTH."
"*Philadelphia, March 28, 1799.*"

The troops quartered at the Spring House[2] tavern and farm houses in the neighborhood the night of April 4, and, the next morning, several cavalry companies resumed the march up the old Bethlehem road[3] for Seller's tavern.[4] This was the

---

[2] The Spring House is on the Bethlehem road, in Gwynedd township, Montgomery county, twenty miles from Philadelphia. It is an old settlement. The inn has been a famous hostelry in its time and was probably licensed as early as 1735. The village consists of a store and a dozen houses. Four incorporated turnpikes meet here. On his pedestrian trip to Niagara, 1804, Alexander Wilson, the ornithologist, stopped over night at the Spring House, and wrote its praise in verse:

"The road was good, the passing scenery gay,
Mile after mile passed unperceived away,
Till in the west the day began to close,
And Spring House tavern furnished us repose,
There two long rows of market folks were seen,
Ranged front to front, the table placed between,
Where bags of meat and bones, and crusts of bread,
And hunks of bacon all around were spread;
One pint of beer from lip to lip went round,
And scarce a crumb the hungry house dog found;
Torrents of Dutch from every quarter came,
Pigs, calves and saurkrout the important theme;
While we, on future plans revolving deep,
Discharged our bills and straight retired to sleep."

[3] The Bethlehem road was originally laid out from the land of Peter Trexler, in the present Lehigh county, then in Bucks, to the Spring House tavern, Philadelphia county, now Montgomery, 1735, by Robert Thomas, John Roberts, Hugh Evans, and Jan Jansen, viewers. It was one of the great arteries of travel for more than a century from Lehigh to Philadelphia, and was tapped by numerous lateral roads. It was gradually extended up the country as the settlements went north, reaching Nathaniel Irish's stone quarry, in the Hellertown road, at Iron Hill, 1738, and Bethlehem and Nazareth, 1745. It crossed the Lehigh a short distance below Bethlehem, at the head of the island now owned by the Bethlehem Iron Company. It was piked in 1805-06. The Old Bethlehem road unites with the New Bethlehem road at Line Lexington.

[4] Sellers' tavern, the present Sellersville, is on the North Penn. railroad, in Rockhill township, Bucks county, and, before the railroad was built, was a noted inn on the Bethlehem road. Philip Henry Zoller was the first of the family to settle in that section, about the middle of the last century. His son, Samuel Sellers, built a house and opened a tavern there, about 1780, a small stone square structure, two stories and an attic. Here his son, Thomas, was born, 1787. On the death of his father he took possession and owned it many years, keeping a store and tavern. He was the first postmaster, 1820; was prominent in affairs, and elected sheriff and to the Legislature. It has had several owners, each occupant making some alterations. After Thomas Sellers came Peter Kneckel, Amos Jacoby, Simon Jacoby, Harry Jacoby &c., down to C. M. Hartzell, the

present Sellersville in Rockhill township,[5] Bucks county, on the line of the North Pennsylvania railroad. They got there that day and encamped on the farm of Andrew Schlichter, which, we believe, is still in the family, and was occupied by a grandson a few years ago. General Macpherson probably did not follow with the main body until the 6th, as his address bears the date of that day. There is, however, a conflict as to the date of its publication, for while the address itself is dated the 6th, the Philadelphia *Daily Advertiser*[6] states it was promulgated on the 5th, the day the cavalry resumed their march. If this date be correct General Macpherson probably marched with the cavalry. The whole force was now assembled at Sellers' tavern, where headquarters was established. Judge Peters arrived at 11 o'clock on Saturday morning to be at hand to bind over, for appearance at court, any persons who might be arrested. General Macpherson appointed Robert Goodloe Harper,[7] Esq., an additional aide-de-camp, and other

present owner. The interior was recently modernized, and a new porch built in front, but the old walls are there. The village was erected into a borough, 1874, and the population is about 1200.

[5] Rockhill, a township in Bucks county, was settled by Germans between 1720 and 1730, and that nationality continues largely the ruling element. It lies in the northwest section of the county and borders Montgomery. The township was organized in 1740, with an area of 14,343 acres, and is one of the most populus townships in the county. Perkasie Manor, a tract of 10,000 acres, granted by William Penn, in trust to his son John, 1701, was partly in Rockhill. The township is well watered and fertile. Sellers' tavern, the first objective point of Macpherson's army, is in Rockhill township.

[6] *The Daily Advertiser*, which had its birth as *The Pennsylvania Packet and General Advertiser*, 1771, and was the first newspaper established in Philadelphia, in the Revolutionary period. Its publisher was John Dunlap, a man of varied abilities and broad enterprise, and took David C. Claypole into partnership. In 1784 it developed into a daily, the first daily newspaper published in America, under the name of *The Daily Advertiser*. It wielded great influence. On September 19, 1796, Washington's farewell address to the people of the United States, first appeared in its columns, the manuscript of which Washington allowed Claypole to retain. During the prevalence of the yellow fever in Philadelphia, in the summer and early fall of 1798, the office of the *Advertiser* was removed to Germantown. The paper ceased to exist many years ago.

[7] Robert Goodloe Harper was born near Fredericksburg, Va., in 1765. For a time he served in the army during the Revolution. He graduated at Princeton, 1785; was admitted to the Bar of Charleston, S. C., 1786; member of Congress, 1794-1801. Served in the War of 1812, being promoted from Colonel to Major-General. He was elected U. S. Senator from Maryland and served in that body, 1816-1821. As an associate of Joseph Hopkinson he participated in the impeachment trial of Judge Chase of the U. S. Supreme Court; in 1821 he became the Federalist candidate for Vice President of the United States. He was an eminent jurist and statesman. He died at Baltimore, January 15, 1825.

arrangements were made to perfect the organization of the troops, and have them in the best possible shape for the war they were about entering on.

From this point the active operations of the campaign were to commence. They were within striking distance of the houses of the leaders of the disturbance in Bucks county, whom they sought to secure. Fries was the first object of capture, and, the same day the troops encamped at Sellers' tavern, a scout was organized to effect his arrest. Some of his acquaintance had given General Macpherson information of his whereabouts, and one, a neighbor, agreed to accompany the troops as guide. The detail for this purpose consisted of four companies of cavalry, two commanded by Captains Porter and Wharton, but the names of the commanders of the other two we have not been able to learn. The troops left camp soon after noon piloted by David Penrose, who lived at Bunker Hill.[8] It was known he was engaged that day to cry a vendue for one Fried at this place, and it was the intention to capture him while thus employed. They continued their march up the old Bethlehem road in the direction of that point.

In the forenoon, when Fries was on his way to the vendue, he passed by the residence of William Edwards, father of the late Caleb Edwards, Quakertown, who, with his son, was making fence along the road. Mr. Edwards told Fries he would be arrested if he went to the vendue, and he had better stay away. He replied he was not afraid, and that no one or two men would take him. Edwards said there would be more than one or two there, but Fries made no reply and continued on his way. He was afoot and accompanied by his little black dog. Mr. Edwards' son soon mounted his father's stallion and rode down to the vendue, where a large number of people were collected; the fact that the troops were expected probably bringing more together than usually assembled at such places. When the troops were first seen ap-

---

[8] Bunker Hill is on the New Bethlehem road, the line between Richland and Rockhill townships, and contains a store and a dozen dwellings. The old inn has been closed many years.

proaching, about half a mile below the tavern, Fries was on the head of a barrel, bell in his hand crying off an article; this he knocked down to the bidder without much ceremony, then jumped to the ground and took to his heels. The commanding officer rode up and ordered the people to stand, but, having become alarmed, they did not heed his order, and broke and ran in all directions, pursued by the troopers. Among the others was one Trumbower, who, choosing to trust to his heels, was chased by a soldier. He made for a fence which he mounted and sprang over, but just at this time the trooper rode up and made a stroke at him with his sabre, which he fortunately avoided and the blow fell upon the fence. The sabre was broken into three pieces, and Trumbower made his escape. The name of the soldier was Owen Foulke, belonging to one of the Philadelphia companies of cavalry. Caleb Edwards ran for his horse which he mounted to ride home; he was stopped by the soldiers; but David Penrose, the guide, coming up, told them to let him go, and he was permitted to ride away.

In the meantime Fries had succeeded in getting away from the crowd, and, for the time being, eluded his persuers. In the confusion, which followed the arrival of the troops and flight of the crowd, it was some little time before an attempt was made to follow him. As none of the command knew him, they had to trust to their guide for his recognition. A search was instituted among those who remained upon the ground and about the premises, and, not finding him, inquiry was made as to the direction he had taken. This information was soon furnished. Upon leaving the vendue ground, Fries made for a nearby swamp, in a meadow on the farm of John Kachline, half a mile from Bunker Hill, where he concealed himself in a bunch of briars. The soldiers distributed themselves through the meadow as he was suspected of being there, and made a thorough search. He would have remained undiscovered, had not the presence of his dog betrayed his hiding place. He offered no resistance. He was brought back to the tavern, when a horse of Samuel Edwards was seized, upon which he was tied and taken under the escort of the troops down to Sellers' tavern, where he was placed in close confinement.

There is a difference of opinion as to the place of capture of Fries. The Philadelphia *Advertiser* of April 8, 1799, in speaking of the affair, states he was taken in a wood and was not secured until after a pursuit of nearly five miles. Our information was obtained from Caleb Edwards, of Quakertown, who was present at the vendue the day of the arrest, and was conversant with all the facts of the case. We think his statement more reliable than that of a newspaper editor who lived at a distance of thirty miles from the scene of action. The same evening a detachment of cavalry from the first and third city troops left camp about sunset to arrest Eberhart, another of the insurgents. He was taken in his own house, in the night, and, of course, made no resistance. The troops called at the houses of several other disaffected persons, but found none of them at home, they having probably fled at their approach. They returned to camp the next morning before day-break, after a ride of between forty and fifty miles. As soon as Eberhart heard of the approach of the troops, he became much alarmed and began to see the danger in which he stood. The day that Fries was taken he called upon Mr. Foulke and begged him to shield him from the military, and pleaded, in extenuation of the opposition he had made to the law, that he was drunk at the time. An officer, who writes from the camp at Sellers' tavern, under date of April 6, says when the capture of Fries was announced, "The joy manifested on this occasion was not to be described; the cheers from the encampment were loud and repeated." The following extract from a letter written at Quakertown, on April 8, considered the matter in a less serious light, and the writer presumed to turn the campaign and capture of Fries into ridicule. The author was probably an officer or soldier of the command although that fact is not stated. He says:

"It will doubtless afford you much satisfaction to hear of the success of our arms against the rebels. Truxton's splendid naval victory must yield to the superior splendor of the late action, which took place on the 5th instant, in the neighborhood of Quakertown. Fries, the noted insurgent leader, who, by profession, is a vendue cryer, and who, on that account, had obtained some ascendency over the multitude, was informed on the morning of the day of the action, (which was a day on which he was also to cry a vendue) that the federal troops were in the neighborhood, and that they were resolved to capture him, and all the world beside if they opposed them. Fries laughed at the account, said he would cry the vendue in spite of the standing army, and seemed to talk as if he was not afraid of them. However, while he was busily engaged in his work of the lungs, to his great surprise he beheld, about half a mile distant, the troops approaching. He carried no arms for his defence but his heels, and, of course, the formidable appearance of a *regular* and *disciplined army* struck him with such a panic he threw down the fire shovel he was crying and made the best of his way to the woods.

" The troops, with uncommon *spirit* and *intrepidity* marched on towards the crowd assembled at the vendue, and, with a menacing air, demanded the leader of the rebels. A boy of about eighteen, never having (I suppose) seen such boldness and intrepidity in military array, fled with uncommon precipitation. Several of the troopers desirous of exhibiting their zeal and activity in the cause of humanity, pursued the poor soul. For some time, by dint of dodging and taking the advantage of fences, he kept them at bay. They grew more and more warm, as the battle increased in difficulty, and at last discharged their pistols at him and shot a hole through his hat ; this brought him to the ground. The troops drew their swords, and it is declared, by a person near the scene of action, that they wounded him severely, and would, no doubt, have killed him, had not some of those that were in the war been informed, that the person captured was not Fries, but a Dutch boy, 18 ! ! ! Fries had a dog—(this dog, no doubt, will be entitled to a commission or a pension for life for his services)— this dog having missed his master was in search of him. Though as rank a rebel as Fries, no doubt, yet it is ten to one, that the sharp-scented warrior would not have smelt his track, and of course he would have escaped, had it not been for his own officers and federal dog. The troops, understanding that Fries had gone such a particular course, and upon some persons among the insurgents panting after him, the troops had the dog as a pilot, till they finally came in sight of the true rebel. Thus was Fries taken by his dog. A dog worth two of Homer's hero's dogs! for he has, in a manner, quelled the formidable insurrection, an insurrection that has called forth the energies of government from all quarters. Now, if this Federal dog is treated according to his merit, he will doubtless obtain an appointment in the army; a troop of dogs under his command might be used to great advantage among the savage Germans, and thus might they obtain new honors equal to the dogs of Cortez in South America."

Another informant says that the night after the arrest of Fries, he was taken to the house of Samuel Thomas, father of the late Edward Thomas, of Quakertown, who lived in Richland township, near Lester's tanyard, on the Bethlehem road, where he was confined in a back room of a brick building standing a few years ago, and probably at this time, and, in 1861, inhabited by Enos P. Nace.

After the capture of John Fries, the military endeavored to make a prisoner of his son, Daniel, an active youth of 18, who was somewhat implicated with his father in his operations. They attempted to capture him at home, but he eluded them and took to the fields and woods. He was chased by the light horse into what was then called "Smith's Meadow." near Swamp Creek.[9] The bogs bore him and he ran across without hindrance, but the horses were too heavy and broke through, one of the riders falling off and breaking his arm. Seeing they could not persue young Fries across the meadow, they turned back and he escaped. During the imprisonment of his father, Daniel went to Philadelphia to be present at the trial and watch events. The authorities, hearing of him be-

---

[9] Swamp Creek rises in Lower Milford township, Lehigh county, a mile from Steinsburg. Several small streams flow into it within a half mile, and it becomes a considerable stream in the neighborhood of Milford Square, where it receives other affluents. It empties into the Perkiomen half a mile below Sumneytown, Montgomery county.

ing in the city, made efforts to arrest him, but in this they were frustrated. Information of what was going on being conveyed to his friends, they concealed Daniel in a joiner's shop, until night, when he quietly left for home and reached it in safety. He was never apprehended. He lived and died near Sumneytown, Montgomery county, where I interviewed him in his 78th year and received these facts from his own lips.

The next day after the arrest of Fries, he was taken before Judge Peters and examined, and what he said was reduced to writing and signed by him. The following is a copy of what was produced at his trial and admitted in evidence against him. The confession is said to have been made voluntarily.

THE EXAMINATION OF JOHN FRIES, APRIL 6, 1799.

"The examinant, confesses that he was one of the party which rescued the prisoners from the Marshal at Bethlehem; that he was also one of a party that took from the assessors, at Quakertown, their papers and forewarned them against the execution of their duty in making the assessments. The papers were delivered with the consent of the assessors, but without force; perhaps under the awe and terror of the numbers who demanded them, and were by this examinant delivered to the assessors. He confesses that, at the house of Jacob Fries, a paper was written on the evening preceding the rescue of the prisoners at Bethlehem, containing an association or agreement of the subscribers to march for the purpose of making that rescue; but he is not certain whether he wrote that paper. He knows he did not sign it, but it was signed by many persons and delivered to the examinant; he does not know where the paper is. The examinant confesses, also, that, some weeks ago, he wrote (before the assessors came into that township) an agreement which he, with others signed, purporting that, if an assessment must be made, they would not agree to have it done by a person who did not reside in the township, but they would choose their own assessor within their township. A meeting has been held in the township since the affair at Bethlehem for the purpose of making such a choice; examinant went to the place of election, but left it before the election opened. The examinant further acknowledges that his motive in going to Bethlehem to rescue the prisoners was not from personal attachment or regard to any of the persons who had been arrested, but proceeded from a general aversion to the law, and an intention to impede and prevent its exaction. He thought that the acts for the assessment and collection of a direct tax did not impose the quota equally upon the citizens and therefore were wrong. He cannot say who originally projected the rescue of the prisoners, or assembled the people for the purpose. The township seemed to be all of one mind. A man, unknown to the examinant, came to Quakertown, and said the people should meet at Conrad Marks' to go to Millarstown. The examinant says that, on the march of the people to Bethlehem, he was asked to take the lead, and did ride on before the people until they arrived at Bethlehem. The examinant had no arms, and took no command, except that he desired the people not to fire until he should give them orders, for he was afraid, as they were so much enraged, there would be bloodshed. He begged them, for God's sake, not to fire, unless they had orders from him, or unless he should be shot down, and then they might take their own command. That he returned the papers of the assessors, which had been delivered into his hands, back to the assessors privately, at which the people were much enraged, and suspected him (Fries) of having turned from them, and threatened to shoot him, between the house of Jacob Fries and Quakertown."

      (Signed)     "JOHN FRIES."
Taken April 6, 1799, before RICHARD PETERS.

As soon as this examination had been taken, Fries and Eberhart were sent off to Philadelphia under the escort of a detachment of the city cavalry, where they arrived the same evening, Saturday, and were lodged in jail to await their trial for treason. Their arrival and commitment were announced in the newspapers the next morning, and created considerable excitement.

The troops broke camp at Sellers' tavern and marched for Quakertown, where they encamped, it is supposed, on the 6th.

They pitched their tents at three different points within the limits of the borough, two campanies being located at Penrose's pottery, belonging to the late Richard Moore. The same evening a detachment of cavalry was despatched in pursuit of persons who were accused of having participated in the late disturbance. They were absent from camp all night, and after a hard scout returned the next morning with several prisoners. It was reported that Clergyman Eyerman was of the number, but this turned out to be a false rumor. He had put himself out of harm's way immediately upon his release at Bethlehem. While the army remained encamped at Quakertown the troops were active in the pursuit of the disaffected, and scouts were sent out in all directions to apprehend them. On the seventh a detachment was sent into the region known as the Rocks,[10] where some of the insurgents resided, and captured several of them, whom they brought to camp, and placed in confinement. The troops remained here until the 8th, when they struck their tents and marched for Millarstown, Northampton county. The presence of the troops at Quakertown inspired terror among the inhabitants in all that region of country, and their conduct caused great distress and suffering. In their zeal to arrest the guilty their displeasure often fell upon the innocent. Armed parties patrolled the country in all directions, day and night, and it was only necessary to cast suspicion upon the most upright citizen to secure his arrest. Many persons took advantage of this state of things to have revenge upon their personal or political enemies. The houses of quiet, unoffending people were entered at the dead hour of night by armed men, and the husband torn from the arms of his wife and screaming children; and their terror was greatly increased by the belief that death awaited those who should be taken, whether they were innocent or guilty. The scenes of distress which took place among these poor people, upon such occasions, are described by the eye-witnesses as heartrendering. In many instances the troops added insult to injury, by exulting over the misfortunes of the poor creatures who had fallen into their

---

[10] The "Rocks" probably refer to the rocky section of Milford township.

hands. So general was the alarm that many of the inhabitants, persons of considerable property and respectable standing, came in and surrendered themselves to the military authorities.

# The Fries Rebellion.

### CHAPTER X.

#### The Army Marches From Quakertown to Allentown, and Returns to Philadelphia via Reading.

While the troops were encamped at Quakertown, and engaged in pursuit of those denounced as insurgents, an alarming system of terror prevailed. This was carried to such extent that a large majority of both officers and men, belonging to the expedition, became dissatisfied and disgusted with the duties they were called upon to perform. An officer thus writes to a friend in Philadelphia, from camp under date of April 8, 1799.

"The system of terror here, I am sorry to say, is carried far beyond what, in my opinion, the public good requires. Detachments are out every day, and night apprehending one or other individuals. I am well informed that from the time the members from this district in the State Legislature went among the people and stated to them the impropriety of interfering with the civil power, the magistrates could have effected everything that government could require in the apprehension of any person in the district. There is scarcely an officer or private in this expedition who is not satisfied of this fact. The scenes of distress which I have witnessed among these poor people, I cannot describe, when we have entered their houses. Conceive your home entered at the dead of night by a body of armed men, and yourself dragged from your wife and screaming children. These poor people are extremely ignorant, but they have feelings, and they always consider that death awaits any one who is seized, be he culpable or not. I am sorry to say there have been any instances of an inhuman disposition exhibited; they have not indeed been many, but vaunting exultation over men, even if they are guilty, when they are captives is neither a proof of generosity or courage. Great numbers of the inhabitants are coming in voluntarily and surrendering themselves; many of them persons of respectable property, and of good standing in the neighborhood."

The following is an extract from another letter, written from the same place while the army was encamped there and of the same date, which will give the reader some idea of the unpleasant state of feeling existing in the section of Bucks county where the disturbance had taken place.

"Some of the townships have been at variance ever since the commencement of our Revolution; and they have been characterized according as they took part for or against Britain, as *Tory* or *Whig* townships; they consist for the most part of Germans. The townships denominated *Tory* have always been attached to Mr. Adam's administration; the others of course had different politics. Much bitterness has been constantly exhibited on both sides; but an ancedote, which occurred on this occasion, will, however, give you a closer view than a general relation. It appears that persons of both descriptions were opposed to the window tax, or rather the *Tories* were opposed to the *tax*, and the *Whigs* to the *assessors*. The landlord of the house in which we were quartered had given information against several of his neighbors who lived in a 'Whig' township, and said they should be hanged together with Fries, but particularly Fries for holding a captain's commissions in the last war. A person present, who heard him make this declaration, supposing he meant in the British service, said it was not so; the landlord replied that it was true, and that a reference to the proceedings of Congress would show it, as well as the name of the Continental battalion in which he served."

Among the letters written from Quakertown, while the troops were encamped there was one giving the name, and number, and persons who were taken, or had surrendered, which breathes quite a belligerent spirit toward the unfortunates implicated, as the following extract will show :

"We are here now two days, and shall proceed immediately to Millarstown; when we reach that place I expect to be permitted to return home. We have been successful since we set out, and shall have a drove of rascals sufficient to fill a jail; we have already taken thirty-one of them; against, which there is sufficient proof to convict of high treason; the others of misdemeanor. Some of them are frightened almost to death; the fear they are in is punishment almost sufficient for the greatest of the offenders. By to-morrow night we shall have about fifty more bad fellows; small fry are admitted to bail. The main guard is pretty well filled.

"Some of the above persons came in and surrendered themselves, by way of making peace, which saved the troops the trouble of going for them, and may save their lives as they expect by it."

The following are the names given and the offences for which they were arrested :

### TREASON.

John Fries, John Everhard, Jacob Huber, John Huber, Frederick Heaney, Christopher Socks, Jacob Klein, Sr., John Klein, Jr., Daniel Klein, Abraham Braith, Jacob Klein, John Getman, George Getman, William Getman and Daniel Weidner.

### MISDEMEANOR.

Aaron Samsel, Peter Hamberg, Abraham Strong, Peter Heidrick, Jacob Huber, Henry Huber, Michael Breich, Abraham Heidrick, Henry Mumbower, George Mumbower, Peter Gable, Jacob Gable and Daniel Gable.

### HELD AS WITNESSES.

George Mitchell and William Thomas.

These sum up fifteen held for treason; fourteen for misdemeanor, and two at witnesses, thirty-one in all. There is hardly a name in the list that cannot be found among the residents of the German districts, of Bucks to-day, and are among the most prosperous, intelligent and respectable citizens.

While this volume was in preparation,* we received a letter from Mr. James C. Iden, an intelligent and highly respectable citizen of Buckingham township, Bucks county, detailing some interesting incidents connected with the Fries Rebellion, from which we make the following extracts. He writes:

"I remember of hearing my mother say, that on the afternoon on which the insurgents marched to Quakertown, and took the assessors, Foulke and Rodrock, prisoners, her father, James Chapman, managing to elude them, arrived unmolested at his home, one mile west of Quakertown, (I think on the farm now occupied by P. Moyer) on the road to Milford Square. But apprehending an attack from Captain Fries and his party, he sent his family to pass the night at one of his neighbors, and then proceeded to barricade the doors and windows of his dwelling, having armed himself with guns, pistols, axes, etc., to repel an attack, should one be made. It proved, however, to be a needless precaution, as no attack was attempted.

"One day, while the military were encamped within the disaffected districts, a company of troops was detailed to make some arrests. The persons, after whom they were sent, having got wind of their approach concluded to leave for parts unknown. Being closely pursued they took refuge under an arched bridge, and the troops rode over and passed them. Waiting a little while they ventured out again and made good their escape. The troops soon finding themselves at fault, and, suspecting how the matter stood, returned to the bridge and searched under it, but were too late as the quarry had flown. They returned to camp quite mortified at their adventure, and declaring it was the last time they would ride over a bridge without examining it thoroughly.

"On another occasion a party was sent out to reconnoitre, but, finding nothing that required their attention, they con-

---

* 1859-60.

cluded to have some sport by shooting at a mark, taking a farmer's wheelbarrow for their target. Being within hearing distance of the camp, the report of their guns produced a great commotion therein, it being supposed they had met with resistance, and probably would send for reinforcements. After waiting on the tiptoe of expectation for some time their trepidation was allayed by the return of the party to quarters, without, however, their having had the honor of receiving any wounds in their country's defense, or bearing with them any of the trophies of war. They and their commander, however, when the cause of the firing was inquired into were fated to have their feelings wounded by a severe reprimand from his superior officer for such a flagrant breach of the rules of military discipline, accompanied by a peremtory order to lay siege to no more wheelbarrows during the campaign.

"Many of the insurgents were arrested and examined as to the extent of their participation. One person, (a German) on being questioned as to whether he had carried arms, replied that he had carried an old mustick (musket,) but she was 'goot fer nossing, she would not *go loose*.' He was asked, 'if so, why did you carry it'? His reply was, 'O, I dunnow—I dought mebby I might schkeer some potty.'"

In the same letter Mr. Iden furnishes us the following sketch of James Chapman, one of the assessors, which we insert at this point for want of a more appropriate place:

"James Chapman, my grandfather, I may say, was born in Springfield township, in October, 1743; that he learned the trade of a cabinet maker, but quit it about the time of his marriage, and commenced farming, surveying and conveyancing, which he followed until age prevented, residing most of the time in the vicinity of Quakertown. After the close of the Revolution he was employed by Judge Wilson, of Penna., Governor Hooper, of N. J., and others, to survey and locate lands for them in what are now Carbon, Monroe, Pike, and Wayne counties. He suryeved and located the State road from Allentown through Mauch Chunk, Wilkesbarre and

Towanda to the State line, (a profile of which I have) also the North and South road leading from the Wind Gap to the State line.

" In locating some lands for himself he entered a tract on the south side of Nesquehoning Valley—the tract lying immediately south of it being the one on which the Lehigh coal mines were afterwards discovered; he giving the preference to the former on account of the quality of the timber, thereby missing, as it were, by a hair's breadth the acquisition of almost boundless wealth. He held the appointment of county surveyor for many years, also the office of director of the poor at the time the almshouse was built in 1808. Some persons urged the directors to build it one story higher, which he opposed, saying that 'the tax-payers of Bucks county would conclude that it was *high* enough by the time it was *paid* for.' He was one of the county commissioners in 1812, when the court house was erected in Doylestown. When his term expired he was appointed clerk to the board of commissioners, which he held until a few months before his death, which occurred near Mechanicsville, in Buckingham township, 1821, aged nearly 78.

" Being noted for his personal appearance, his weight being 270 pounds, and also for his great sociability and fund of anecdote and ready repartee, in connection with the length of his public life, there were comparatively few residents of the county at that day to whom he was not known; persons of all ages and conditions addressing him by the familiar title of 'Uncle Jimmy Chapman.' The generation to which he belonged, have now nearly all passed away; the venerable Nathaniel Shewell,[1] of Doylestown township, being the only survivor of his friends and associates, who now remains with us at the advanced age of nearly 100 years."*

---

[1] Nathaniel Shewell, a leading character of his generation in Bucks county, a descendant of Walter Shewell, who came from Gloucestershire, England, 1732, and settled in what is now Doylestown township. He built a handsome dwelling on a tract he purchased and called it " Painswick Hall," after his birth place. Betsy Shewell, the wife of Benjamin West, was a member of the family. Mr. Shewell was elected sheriff of the county, 1800, serving a full term of three years, and was appointed county treasurer, 1820. Mr. Shewell died at the close of 1860, his will being proved January 2, 1861.

*About 1859-60.

The army remained in camp at Quakertown until April 8, when the march was resumed toward Bethlehem, Northampton county, in which region of country there were many insurgents whose arrest was desired. On that day they marched but ten miles, when they again halted, and encamped, as some arrests were to be made in that neighborhood. It was a great relief to the inhabitants of Quakertown and the surrounding country when the army left that place, and many a prayer that they might never return was offered up. The absence of the soldiers and harassing scouts soon restored the usual quiet in that section of the country, although the interest in the campaign was still kept up. Of the prisoners named, 19 were sent to Philadelphia, under an escort of cavalry commanded by Lieutenant Melbecke, where they arrived on Thursday, the 18th inst., and were turned over to the civil authorities. Conrad Marks, who will be rembered as an active participant in Bucks county, surrendered himself on the 17th to the deputy marshal. A writ had been issued for his arrest, and several parties of cavalry were sent in pursuit of him, but he eluded them all, and, at last, thought proper to give himself up. He offered bail but it was refused, and he was sent to the city and thrown into prison.

The army now proceeded to Millarstown, Lehigh county, where they again encamped, reaching this place probably on the 10th. We have no means of knowing how long they remained there, but probably did not leave before about the 16th. While encamped here they were joined by two more troops of horse, and a column of infantry. A grand review and inspection was held, and the troops are said to have presented a very handsome appearance. From this point parties of cavalry were sent out in pursuit of the insurgents, and some arrests were made, but neither the number nor names is given. It is related that one of the captured was brought before a well known magistrate and was anxious to know the fate that awaited him, to which the official replied with becoming dignity, "in a fortnight the Circuit Court will meet, when you will be tried, and, in a fortnight after, will be in hell, sir." This circumstance is mentioned to show the bitterness of the times, more than for any other purpose. Many excesses were also committed while the troops lay at Millarstown, and the same system of terror was maintained. An officer writing from camp under date of April 11, says:

"With respect to military operations, they still continue; and the number of persons confined in heavy irons increases. I before mentioned to you that some old men have suffered from their fetters. Several of them, who have been thus accoutred, marched through the county under a heavy guard. Bail to any amount has been offered for their appearance to take their trial, but this would not suit the system of terror, nor would it act as a warning to those who may be disposed to vote as they think best at the next election. All the efforts that have been made, however, will not produce resistance, and when I tell you that a number of the troops who derive their authority from the Federal government, live at free quarters on the people, you will not question their patience."

Another officer writing from the same place, under date of April 10, thus speaks of the expedition, and the unhappy situation of things while the army remained in the country:

"We are now quartered in a Whig town where the people have always been true Republicans. It appears now to be converted into an actual war between Whig and Tory. The people of Quakertown I find have always been opposed to those who advocate arbitrary measures, and the funding system and standing army. This place, however, appears to have been one of the places where the greatest opposition has been made to the assessors, who, being many of them engaged in hostility against the revolution must, of necessity, have excited disgust and abhorrence in the breast of those who had fought, or whose fathers had bled, in fighting against the British. The inhabitants are principally Germans. Nearly all the male inhabitants, on the approach of our army, fled from their homes, and their wives and children exhibit a very unhappy scene of distress. Had I conceived that some things, which I have witnessed here could have taken place, I should never have given my assent to march a mile on the expedition.

"One effect produced by the distress is that every individual, whom I meet, is disgusted, and a sentiment generally prevails, which, contrary to expectation, will, I apprehend, completely destroy the federal influence at the next election. Had the Governor seconded Messrs. Hartzell, and the Senator from this district, by ordering a single troop of volunteer horse that is here under drums, I am persuaded that this business, of which so much has been made, would have terminated within the 24 hours that it took place; and that no other weapons than reasoning would have been found necessary. Great numbers of the people have surrendered; there are about seven detained in irons and I am grieved to see among them some old men, whose wrists are raw to the bone with the hand-cuffs. I would wish to see more humanity among my countrymen, but, unhappily we copy too much the cruel and unfeeling practices of the English.

"A liberty pole had been erected in this place, which was cut down by force on the approach of the army. The inn-keeper, near whose house it stood, was arrested when we came up, although he had been previously at Philadelphia and given bail; but, when a volunteer army proceeds thus what would the people have to fear from mercenaries, who have no interest at stake, no principle but obedience to arbitrary orders."

A third letter written from the same point, says:

"There are several of these poor creatures who are implicated by information, stirred up in the neighborhood, from the embers of old quarrels and animosities, whose distress is very great. Numbers of them, I am informed, are willing to give themselves up, relying on their innocence, provided they were sure of being admitted to bail; but it is generally understood they will not. Pray, is there no magistrate in the city who has authority to receive bail? Is there no one who feels a sentiment that justice is incompatible with cruelty, and that the mildness of our laws does not authorize the infliction of severe punishment before trial and execution? I can scarcely persuade myself that I tread on the soil of Pennsylvania when I witness the sufferings of these poor, well-meaning, but ignorant, Germans. They are treated in no respect like citizens of the same country."

The army marched from Millarstown to Allentown, the present county seat of Lehigh, by way of Bethlehem,[2] but we cannot fix the exact date of leaving Millarstown. It was after April 15, for the troops were there then. They remained at Allentown only a few days, and, while there, do not appear to have been as active in making arrests and committing excesses as at other points. While the army lay here an amusing occurrence took place which is thus related by one who belonged to the expedition:

"One night a sentinel, stationed near a wagon, reported that he heard some person about to make an attack upon it. The alarm was given, the drums beat to arms, and the whole command turned out. The arms were loaded with ball cartridge, and a member of Congress was sent out to reconnoitre, who, upon his return, reported that the enemy (insurgents) were in rear of the baggage in great force. The troops marched to the point, and a platoon was ordered to fire, when a heavy groan was heard, and a body fell to the earth. Some of the boldest ventured forward, and behold they had shot a bull which was making free with the forage that hung out of the tail of one of the wagons. The animal was paid for. This is believed to be the only thing the army killed on the expedition."

From Allentown the troops marched to Reading, in Berks county, by the way of Greenmeyer and Karackerstown, where they arrived on Saturday, April 20, at one o'clock. Writs had been issued for the arrest of sixteen persons in Greenmeyer township, but fourteen of them came in and surrendered

---

[2] Jacob Rice, of Bethlehem, in a note to the author, on the march of the army from Millarstown says: "The troops marched from Millarstown to Allentown, which lies northeast from the first named place, about 8 miles. Bethlehem lies due east from Allentown, distance 6 miles, consequently their route was not by way of Bethlehem. The troops, with the exception of a few horse, never came to Bethlehem."

themselves, and the troops were sent in pursuit of the other two, but they could not be found. The army made no stay at this place, but almost immediately resumed the march for Philadelphia, where a portion of the cavalry arrived on the 22d, and the remainder, with General Macpherson, the next day. The regulars did not return to the seat of government at the same time as the volunteer corps, but remained encamped there for a while.

While the army was in Reading, the members of one of the troops of volunteer cavalry committed a gross outrage upon the person of one of the most respectable citizens of the town, without the least cause or provocation, which created great indignation in the community. This consisted in forcibly taking Jacob Schneider, the editor of the Reading *Adler*[3] to the market house, and publicly whipping him, by the order of their captain. The following is Mr. Schneider's own account of the affair, taken from the *Adler* of April 22, 1799.

"On Saturday afternoon last, the troops, who were sent to seize upon some people in Northampton, called 'insurgents,' on their return from that expedition, arrived in this town, and last night and this morning they all, except the regulars, marched for their respective homes.

"It is an old proverb, but certainly a true one, that in every fold, be it great or small, there can be found rotten sheep, so it happened here. This army was small, yet it was not without its rotten members, and some extremely so. But among the whole there were none that exceeded Captain Montgomery's troop, of Lancaster Light Horse, not because, as

---

[3] The Reading *Adler* is the oldest German newspaper published in the United States, having been established November 6, 1796, by Jacob Schneider and George Gerrish. The second number was issued January 10, 1797, and each successive number of the paper has been issued every week to the present time, without a single omission, covering a period of a hundred years. In 1802, John Ritter, nephew of the senior member of the firm and a practical printer, was substituted for Mr. Gerrish. From 1843 to 1847, Mr. Ritter represented the county in Congress, and died in 1851, aged 73. The Ritter family had a continuous interest in the paper from 1802 to 1857, a period of fifty-five years. Other changes have taken place in the proprietorship, the last in 1874, when it fell to the possession of William S. Ritter. The *Adler* is a paper of great influence among the Germans, and a political power in the county. The *Reading Eagle*, a daily published by Jesse G. Hawley, may be called a child of the *Adler*.

they boasted themselves, it was their trade to catch rebels and abuse them—but because they carried their trade so far as to enter the houses and abuse peaceable and inoffending citizens, in a manner the most scandalous and cowardly.

"As for example a part of them came to my printing office on Saturday last, not as men of character desirous of supporting the law and the security of the peaceable citizens, but like a banditti of robbers and assassins. They tore the clothes from my body, and forcibly dragged me from my house before their captain, who certainly proved himself worthy the command of his corps. He ordered his troops to take me to the public market house and give me twenty-five lashes on the bare back, and they proceeded to obey his orders accordingly, and certainly would have fulfilled them exactly had not some of Captain Leiper's troop, of Philadelphia, interfered, reproached them for their illegal and tyrannical conduct, in consequence of which only a part of the sentence of Captain Montgomery (six lashes) was inflicted."

Complaint of this outrage was made to General Macpherson by Colonel Heister[1] and Colonel Frailly, but he did nothing, and no redress could be had. Mr. Schneider was anti-Federalist.

The prisoners in custody were confined in the common jail of the city of Philadelphia, until their trial. It is said their confinement was made unusually severe, and that an order was issued that none of their families, or friends, should be permitted to visit or hold intercourse with them, which was carried into effect.

The expedition, so far as its object, was to arrest those who had disturbed the public peace in the counties of Bucks and Northampton, had been entirely successful, and the leaders of the so-called insurrection were in the hands of the Federal authorities. The next step in the drama, or farce, for we hardly know which to call it, was the trial, condemnation and execution of the prisoners; and the preliminaries to

---

[1] The Heisters are an old and influential family of Berks and Lancaster counties, and have furnished one Governor to the State, Joseph Heister, elected in 1814.

this finâle were urged with as much haste as common decency would permit. For an account of the proceedings attendant on the trial we refer our readers to the next chapter, where it will be as fully recounted as time and space will permit.

# The Fries Rebellion.

## CHAPTER XI.

### Trial of John Fries.

The trial of John Fries was the most extraordinary judicial proceeding our country ever witnessed. The political rancour, which had raged with such fierceness during the closing scenes of the administration of Mr. John Adams, was carried upon the bench and into the jury box, and aided, no doubt, to determine the law and the facts of this case. The Judge evinced an apparent disposition to carry out the high handed measures which had been begun, and whether intentional or not, leaned with a strong bias against the accused.

The Circuit Court of the United States, before which Fries and the other prisoners were to be tried, commenced its session at Philadelphia, on April 11, 1799, the Hon. James Iredell,[1] one of the Associate Justices of the Supreme Court of the United States, being upon the bench. The case was attracting such wide-spread interest, the court room was filled with an excited and deeply interested multitude, as soon as the doors were thrown open. After the court was duly opened for business, Judge Iredell delivered his charge to the

---

[1] James Iredell was of Irish ancestry, born in Lewes, county of Sussex, England, October 5, 1751. His father was a merchant in Bristol. Iredell settled at Edenton, N. C., 1768; studied law and was admitted to the bar, 1770. He was appointed to the Supreme Court of the State, 1777, and Attorney General, 1779. In 1790 Washington appointed him one of the Justices of the Supreme Court of the United States, and he held that office to his death, 1799. He exerted a strong influence in favor of the Revolution, although he did not take an active part at the beginning of the controversy—while at the bar he aided much in giving tone and order to the judicial system of the State.

grand jury, a production which was characterized by great partisan bitterness. He reviewed, at considerable length, the Alien and Sedition Laws, argued their constitutionality, and said they were called for by the spirit of the times. He next passed to the case of Fries, which he noticed with considerable particularity. He contended, in advance of the trial, and in the absence of testimony to sustain his opinion, that the crime with which he stood charged was *Treason;* which, he said, consisted in opposing, by force of arms, the execution of any acts of Congress. The case was given to the grand jury, which retired to their room, where they made such examination of it as was necessary to satisfy their minds of the nature of the offence. When they returned into court they presented a true bill as against John Fries, who now stood indicted for Treason, the highest crime known to our law. The following is a copy of the indictment under which he was to be tried, viz:

*Indictment in the Circuit Court of the United States of America, in and for the Pennsylvania District of the Middle Circuit:*

" The Grand Inquest of the United States of America, for the Pennsylvania District, upon their respective oaths and affirmations, do present that John Fries, late of the county of Bucks, in the district of Pennsylvania, he being an inhabitant of, and residing in the said United States, to wit, in the district aforesaid, and under the protection of the laws of the said United States, and owing allegiance and fidelity to the same United States, not having the fear of God before his eyes, nor weighing the duty of his said allegiance and fidelity, but being moved and seduced by the instigation of the Devil, wickedly devising and intending the peace and tranquility of the said United States to disturb, on March 7, in the year of our Lord one thousand seven hundred and ninety-nine, at Bethlehem, in the county of Northampton, in the district aforesaid, unlawfully, maliciously and traitorously did compass, imagine and intend to raise and levy war, insurrection and rebellion against the said United States; and to fulfil and bring into effect the said traitorous compassings, imaginations and intentions of him the said John Fries, he the said John Fries, afterwards, that is to say, on March seventh, in the said year of our Lord, one thousand seven hundred and ninety-nine, at the said county of Northampton, in the district aforesaid, with a great multitude of persons, whose names at present are unknown to the Grand Inquest aforesaid, to a great number, to wit, to the number of one hundred persons and upwards, armed and arrayed in a warlike manner, that is to say, with guns, swords, clubs, stones, and other warlike weapons, as well offensive as defensive, being then and there unlawfully, maliciously and traitorously assembled and gathered together, did falsely and traitorously assemble, and join themselves together against the said United States, and, then and there, with force and arms, did falsely and traitorously, and in a warlike manner, array and dispose them against the said United States, and then and there, with force and arms, in pursuance of such their traitorous intentions and purposes aforesaid, he, the said John Fries, with the said persons so as aforesaid traitorously assembled, and armed and arrayed in the manner aforesaid, most wickedly, maliciously and traitorously did ordain, prepare and levy public war against the said United States, contrary to the duty of his said allegiance and fidelity, against the Constitution, peace and dignity of the said United States, and also against the force of the Act of the Congress of the said United States, in such case made and provided. (Signed) "WILLIAM RAWLE,"[2]

"Attorney of the U. S. for the Pennsylvania District."

The case was not immediately taken up, but other business on the docket occupied the time of the Court until April 30, when it was called up in order. Fries had employed eminent counsel to defend him, viz: Hon. Alex. J. Dallas,[3] father of

---

[2] William Rawle, born in Philadelphia, April 28, 1759, completed his law studies at the Middle Temple, London, and returning to Philadelphia, 1783, was admitted to the bar. In 1791 he was appointed U. S. District Attorney for Pennsylvania by Washington. He was one of the original members of the Franklin Institute and Historical Society of Pennsylvania, Chancellor of the Law Association; a fine classical scholar, a deeply read and learned jurist and writer of ability. He died April 12, 1836.

[3] Alexander J. Dallas was born in the Island of Jamaica, June 21, 1759; was educated in London, and studied law at the Temple; arrived in Philadelphia with his wife, June 17, 1783, was admitted and began the practice of the law. He rose rapidly in his

Vice President Dallas, and Messrs. Ewing and Lewis.[4] The United States were represented by Messrs. Rawle and Sitgreaves, the latter being a resident of Easton, in Northampton county, and at that time the United States Attorney for the Pennsylvania district. As soon as the case was called up, Mr. Lewis preferred the following motion, in writing, viz:

"And now the prisoner, John Fries, being placed at the bar of this Court, at the city of Philadelphia, being the place appointed by law for holding the stated sessions thereof, and it being demanded of him if he is ready for his trial for the treason in the indictment mentioned, he moves, *oretenus*, that his trial for the same offence may not be proceeded on here, and that the same may be had in the county in which the same acts of treason in the said indictment mentioned are laid, and where the offence therein mentioned is alleged to have been committed."

This motion was argued at length by Messrs. Dallas, Lewis and Ewing. The application was founded on the judiciary act, passed September 24, 1789, the 29th section of which provides, "That in cases punishable with death, the trial shall be had in the county where the offence was committed; or where that cannot be done without great inconvenience, twelve petit jurors at least shall be summoned from thence." Messrs. Sitgreaves and Rawle replied on the part of the United States; when the Court overruled the motion, both judges delivering opinions upon the points raised. One of the reasons given by Judge Iredell why the prisoner should not be tried in the county where the offence was committed was, that the inhabitants were in such a state of insurrection, that a fair trial could not be had. All motions being now disposed of, the next thing in order was to fix a time for the trial, which was set down for the first day of May.

---

profession, and, in 1801, was appointed District Attorney of the United States by President Jefferson. In October, 1814, he accepted the portfolio of the Treasury in the Cabnent of President Maddison. He died at Trenton, N. J., January 14, 1817.

[4] William Lewis was born on a farm in Chester county, 1751, and commenced the study of the law without previous educatian to fit him for it. His preceptor was Nicholas Waln, and became his partner after admission. He has been accorded the highest place among his contemporaries, in spite of his roughness of speech. He drafted the famous Act of 1780, abolishing slavery. He died at Philadelphia in his 70th year.

The prisoner being brought in and placed at the bar of the Court on that day, was duly arraigned; when the indictment was read to him, to which he pleaded "Not Guilty," and placed himself upon his country for trial. A jury was then called and empanelled, which consisted of the following persons: William Jolly, Philadelphia; Samuel Mitchell, and Richard Leedom,[6] Bucks county; Anthony Cuthbert, Alexander Fullerton, John Singer, Philadelphia; Willlam Ramsey,[6] Bucks; Samuel Richards, Philadelphia; Gerardus Wynkoop,[7] Bucks; Jos. Thornton, Philadelphia; Philip Walter, Northampton; John Rhoad, Northampton.

A question arose as to the last two jurymen being qualified, as they were Germans, and did not understand English, but it was agreed that any dfficulty of that nature could be explained to them. Several of the witnesses being also Germans, and not able to speak English, a Mr. Erdman was, on that account, sworn as interpreter.

Mr. Sitgreaves opened the case on the part of the United States. He said, "Treason is defined in the Constitution of the United States, section III., art. III.," in the words following: "Treason against the United States shall consist only in levying war against them, or in adhering to their enemies, giving them aid and comfort." He charged that Fries was guilty of treason in levying war. He then proceeded to elaborate upon the phræsology or description as adopted in our

---

[6] Richard Leedom settled at the "Black Bear," now Richborough, Northampton township, Bucks county, over a century and a half ago, where he hept store many years. His stone dwelling is still standing. He became a prominent man. In his day the place was called "Leedoms," and is situated on the Middle road, 19 miles from Philadelphia.

[6] The Ramseys, of Warwick, Bucks county, are descended from William, a staunch Scotch-Irish Presbyterian, who was born in Ireland, 1698, and came to America, 1741. He had several children, among whom was a William, probably the person mentioned in the text—Robert Ramsey four years in Congress from Bucks county, was a member of this family.

[7] The Wynkoops, a prominent family in Bucks county a century ago, are descended from Cornelius C. Wynkoop, an immigrant from Holland to New York before 1700. They came into Bucks prior to 1750. Gerardus Wynkoop was the son of Gerrit, and an officer of the Revolution. He was a member of the Assembly for nineteen years, and long its Speaker. He died about 1812. Henry Wynkoop was a member of Congress, 1789, and on intimate terms with Washington.

Constitution, which is borrowed from the statute of Great Britain, passed in the reign of Edward the III., and which had never been changed. He then passed to an exposition of the full meaning of the word treason, as understood under our Constitution, and pointed out what is necessary to constitute the crime; and that, according to the definition of Lord Hale, it must consist both in levying war, and in levying war against the government of the United States—that if the people assembled in this hostile manner only to gratify a spirit of revenge, or for any other purpose independent of war against the United States, it would only amount to a riot. He reviewed, at considerable length, the leading operations of Fries and his friends, pointing out their combination and conspiracy to resist the federal authorities, and their actual resistance, with arms in their hands, at Bethlehem. He now called witnesses to prove the facts stated in his opening. Among those subpœnæd and called upon the stand were, William Henry, William Barnett, John Barnett, Christian Winters, Christian Roths, Colonel Nichols, Philip Sclaugh, Joseph Horsefield, John Mohollon, Jacob Eyerley, Samuel Toon, George Mitchell, Wm. Thomas, James Chapman, John Rodrock, Cephas Childs and others. In the main their testimony sustained the facts alleged by Mr. Sitgreaves, and most if not all the overt acts set forth in the indictment were substantially proved.

Among the witnesses called was Judge Peters, then upon the bench, who was examined more particularly as to the circumstances under which he issued warrants in Northampton county, and in relation to other facts within his knowledge previous to the examination of John Fries, on April 6. At this stage of the trial the confession of Fries was read, the same which was taken before Judge Peters, immediately upon his capture, and which was printed in a previous chapter.

The prosecution having now rested their case, Mr. Dallas remarked to the Court, that, though they wished to give as little trouble on the part of the defendant as possible, they desired to call two or three witnesses to prove that the indisposition which was manifested to permit the assessments to be made was owing to the uncertainty these people were in of the real existence of the law; that the prisoner himself was under the idea that it was no law; and that they had no intention of opposing Congress by force of arms, but that they wished for time, in order to ascertain its real existence, and, if the law were actually in force, they wished, agreeably to their former custom, to appoint assessors from their own respective townships; that it could be shown that Fries was perfectly quiescent after the proclamation, and that some of the witnesses were mistaken as to some of the facts which they had sworn to. Mr. Dallas alluded to the fact, that since the jury had been impanneled, a newspaper in the city had attempted to intimidate the counsel and jury, to warp the sentiments of the latter, and to deprive the prisoner of the benefit of the best talent the bar could afford. He proceeded to an examination of the law of treason, and argued that none of the acts complained of amounted to the crime charged.

After Mr. Rawle had argued the constitutional definition of treason to the Court, in support of the positions taken by his colleague, Mr. Sitgreaves, Mr. Dallas opened the case for the defendant in an able and eloquent speech. He reviewed the whole ground, all the testimony of the witnesses produced by the United States, and denied that from the facts proved there was anything like the levying of war against the United States. He argued that treason could not be made out of the act alleged, and that at most it was but a conspiracy to resist the execution of an unpopular law. He explained the disadvantages under which the prisoner appeared before the Court, and spoke of the popular resentment that had been engendered against him; and he called upon the jurors to drive from their minds everything like bias, and to give the prisoner the advantage of every reasonable doubt they might entertain of his guilt. Having concluded, he called three witnesses, John Jamison, Israel Roberts and Everhard Folke, to prove the facts he had alleged.

The testimony on both sides being closed, Mr. Ewing opened the case to the jury for the defendant, and was followed by Mr. Sitgreaves and Mr. Rawle, for the United States. The jury was then charged by both Judges at considerable length, who reviewed all the facts of the case, and the law bearing upon it, showing a strong bias against the prisoner. The case was then given to the jury which retired to their room, and after an absence of about three hours came in with a verdict of *Guilty*. The trial had occupied the undivided attention of the Court from the first to the ninth of May, and during all this period the public mind was in the greatest possible state of excitement, and the attendance upon the trial large. The jury did not separate the whole time. When the verdict was announced, it was received with satisfaction or disapprobation, according to the political bias of the persons present; for, strange as it may seem, politics was mixed up with the whole of the affair.

The Court met on the 14th of May to pronounce sentence upon the prisoner. As soon as Court was opened, Mr. Lewis, one of the counsel for Fries, asked for a rule to show cause why a new trial should not be granted, which caused judgment to be suspended, and the prisoner was remanded back to prison. The ground upon which this motion was based, was that John Rhoads, one of the jurymen on the trial, had declared a prejudice against the prisoner after he was summoned as a juror on the trial. He read depositions to substantiate the facts stated. Mr. Lewis was sustained in the application by Mr. Dallas, who advanced additional reasons for a new trial. The motion was argued at considerable length by counsel, and the two judges delivered separate opinions. The Court was divided in opinion, Judge Iredell being in favor of, and Judge Chase[8] opposed to, a new trial; but the latter

---

[8] Samuel Chase, a signer of the Declaration of Independence, was born in Md., April 17, 1741, and died June 19, 1811. He became an eloquent advocate and learned lawyer. He rendered valuable services during the Revolution; was Chief Justice of Md., member of the Maryland Convention for considering the Federal Constitution, and, in 1796, Washington appointed him Associate Justice of the Supreme Court of the United States.

finally yielded to the former upon the ground that a division in the Court might lessen the weight of the judgment if finally pronounced, and a new trial was accordingly granted. Before the second trial came off the yellow fever broke out in Philadelphia, which caused a removal of the prisoners to Montgomery county for greater protection against the malignant disease and where they remained until the fever had abated, when they were returned to Philadelphia.* The late Hon. James M. Porter,° of Easton, wrote us the following interesting recollections of his residence at Norristown, at that period, which we publish in full:

" I was very young at the time of those transactions, but I still have a recollection that they transpired When the yellow fever prevailed in Philadelphia, I think in 1799, Isaiah Wells, Esq., was sheriff of Montgomery (perhaps jailor at that,) and the prisoners were removed from Philadelphia to Norristown. Mr. Wells was very kind and allowed the prisoners great liberties, in going out and returning to the jail. Several of them, if not all, were farmers and accustomed to work on their own properties at home; he allowed them to get work and be paid for it, in order to get pocket money, and have exercise; but required them always to be in the jail at night. One, whose name was Moyer, worked one day for my father, who lived about one mile from the jail. I remember the fact of his working there very distinctly—splitting wood. We had nothing but iron wedges, and this Mr. Moyer was the first person I ever saw use wooden wedges or gluts in splitting the

---

In 1804 he was impeached for misdemeanor in the conduct of several political trials, including that of John Fries, but was acquitted, and resumed his place on the Bench, which he retained until his death.

* A session of the Court was held at Norristown, commencing October 11, 1799, owing to the yellow fever prevailing in Philadelphia, and the case of John Fries was called but not tried at that time. His second trial was afterward had in Philadelphia when the fever had abated.

° James Madison Porter, was born at Selma, Pa., in January of 1793. He served in the Second War with England; studied law, was admitted to the Bar at Easton, 1813, where he became a resident. He took an active part as member of the Constitutional Convention of Pennsylvania, 1838; was appointed Secretary of War, 1843, but rejected by the Senate. He was a founder of Lafayette College, Easton, 1826, and President of its Board of Trustees. He died November 11, 1862.

wood. In the evening he complained of not being very well, and our family wished him to remain all night. This he declined, saying that Mr. Wells was very good to them, but he had desired them to be there every night, and he would be as good as his word. The next day he got worse with the jail fever and died with it at Norristown."

The second trial of John Fries was had in the Circuit Court of the United States, at Philadelphia, which commenced on April 29, 1800. Judge Chase presiding, assisted by Judge Peters, of the District Court. The former indictment had been withdrawn, by the District Attorney, and a new one drawn in its stead, upon which Fries was arraigned and, as before, plead, "Not Guilty." Mr. Dallas and Mr. Lewis, who were engaged on the first trial as counsel for the prisoner, were retained to defend him also upon the second; but they withdrew from the case at the commencement, because of the extraordinary course of the Judges in laying down their opinions as to the law before hearing counsel, thus prejudicing the case. They alleged that this preceeding was not only illegal but wholly unprecedented, and they therefore declined to have anything more to do with the case. This conduct of Judge Chase afterward became the subject of the first of the articles of his impeachment, on which he was tried before the United States Senate, in February, 1805. Their withdrawal left Fries without legal assistance. The Court asked him if he wished to have counsel assigned him, but, as he did not express any desire for it, the trial went on in the absence of it. Mr. Rawle and Mr. Ingersol conducted the prosecution.

Of the jurors called, thirty-four were challenged without cause, and the following were admitted and sworn, viz: Samuel Wheeler, foreman; Henry Pepper, John Taggart, Cornelius Comegys, Ephraim Clark, Thomas Baily, Lawrence Cauffman, John Edge, Charles Deshler, Henry DuBois, Isaac Dehaven, and John Balliott. Before the jurors were sworn, they were individually asked, upon oath, "Are you any way related to the prisoner," to which they all answered "No."

great propriety, but, after the verdict was rendered, he became much affected; and in view of his impending fate remained depressed in spirits down to the time of his liberation. It is said that he confidently expected an acquittal, based on the opinion of his counsel that his offence did not amount to treason.

After the rendition of the verdict, Judge Chase remarked to the prisoner that as he had no counsel on the trial, if he, or any person for him, could point out any flaw in the indictment, or legal ground for arrest of judgment, ample time would be allowed for that purpose. The Court met on Frinay, May 2, to sentence the prisoner. The sentence was pronounced by Judge Chase, who addressed Fries at length, remarking to the other prisoners at the bar, that what he should say to him would apply generally to them. He reviewed the offence of which he had been convicted, after a fair and impartial trial, and pointed out the enormity of the crime in resisting the acts of a government so free and liberal as that of the United States. He called his attention to his near approach to the close of his career on earth, and besought him to prepare for that other life which was beyond the grave. He entreated him to employ the balance of his days in repenting of his sins, and in seeking that pardon which God alone can give. In conclusion, Judge Chase said:

"What remains for me is a very necessary but a very painful part of my duty: it is to pronounce that judgment which the law has appointed for crimes of this magnitude. The judgment of the law is and this Court does award, that you be hanged by the neck *until dead*,' and I pray God Almighty to be merciful to your soul.'"

Samuel Sitgreaves, who conducted the prosecution at the first trial of John Fries, was one of the ablest men Pennsylvania ever produced. He was born in Philadelphia 1763, where he studied law and was admitted to the bar. He removed to Easton, Northampton county about 1786, and, by reason of his great abilities immediately took a high position at the bar, and became prominent in politics. His first appearance in public life, was as a member of the Constitutional Convention of Pennsylvania, 1790, in which he took an active part. He was elected to Congress, 1794, and served until 1798. In the impeachment of Senator Blount, of Tennessee, before the United States Senate, he was one of the leading managers, and discharged his duties with great power, talents and fidelity. In 1799 Mr. Sitgreaves went to England as Commissioner under Jay's treaty, and was absent at the time of the second trial of Fries. After the election of Mr. Jefferson he retired from politics and devoted himself to his profession. He became disgusted with the Federalists, but could not affiliate with the Democrats. He spent the balance of his days in retirement.

During the time that John Fries was confined in prison he received much sympathy from the citizens of Philadelphia, and others. Among those, who took deep interest in his fate, was the Rev. Dr. Janeway, an eminent clergymen of that day, who visited him by permission of the authorities, and ministered to him spiritual and other consolation. He presented him a handsome Bible, of duodecimo size, with which to console his hours of confinement. After his sentence to death, May 9, and when he expected shortly to be led to the scaffold for execution, he made a bequest of this Bible to his children, as follows, viz:

"PHILADELPHIA, May 22, 1800."

"MY DEAR CHILDREN. This Book, presented to me by J. J. Janeway, at his request, I leave as the legacy of your dying father. Let me entreat you to regard it as the best gift of Heaven; as revealing the only way of salvation for lost sinners. I beseech, I command you to read and to study it. I pray that the spirit of God may open your eyes, that you may read it in faith, to the salvation of your immortal souls.
(Signed) "JOHN FRIES."

The Bible is now in possession of John Fries' descendants, who live in Whitemarsh, Montgomery county, and is cherished by them as a great treasure. The bequest is in his hand

"Have you ever formed or delivered an opinion as to the guilt or innocence of the prisoner, or that he ought to be punished;" to which they generally answered not to their knowledge. Some of them admitted that they had spoken in disapprobation of the transaction, but not as to the prisoner particularly. Mr. Taggart, after he was sworn, remarked to the Court that he felt uneasy under his oath, inasmuch as he had often spoken of the prisoner as very culpable, but that he had never made up his mind to hang him; that when he took the oath he did not conceive it to be so strict, and therefore he wished to be excused. The Court informed him that as he was now sworn, it was impossible to excuse him, and he accordingly took his seat with the others.

Mr. Rawle opened the case on the part of the United States. Before any of the testimony was admitted for the prosecution, Judge Chase cautioned the prisoner to attend to the examination of the witnesses against him, and to ask them any questions he might deem proper, but to be careful not to ask any question that might possibly criminate himself. He said that the Court would be watchful of him, and would check anything that might go to injure him, and would be his counsel and grant him every assistance and indulgence in their power. The testimony was much the same as that produced upon the first trial, and sustained the facts laid in the indictment. The prisoner offered no evidence. Mr. Rawle summed up the testimony, briefly, after which Judge Chase charged the jury.

The jury retired about six o'clock in the evening, when the Court adjourned until ten. When they entered the jury room, the jurors agreed, that without previous argument among themselves, the opinion of each one should be expressed by ballot, which was done, and they were unanimously in favor of conviction. At the hour to which they had adjourned, the Court again assembled, when the jury was brought in and delivered the verdict of *Guilty*, amid the most profound silence. During the trial, Fries was tranquil, and bore himself with great propriety, but, after the verdict was rendered, he became much affected; and in view of his impending fate remained depressed in spirits down to the time of his liberation. It is said that he confidently expected an acquittal, based on the opinion of his counsel that his offence did not amount to treason.

After the rendition of the verdict, Judge Chase remarked to the prisoner that as he had no counsel on the trial, if he, or any person for him, could point out any flaw in the indictment, or legal ground for arrest of judgment, ample time would be allowed for that purpose. The Court met on Frinay, May 2, to sentence the prisoner. The sentence was pronounced by Judge Chase, who addressed Fries at length, remarking to the other prisoners at the bar, that what he should say to him would apply generally to them. He reviewed the offence of which he had been convicted, after a fair and impartial trial, and pointed out the enormity of the crime in resisting the acts of a government so free and liberal as that of the United States. He called his attention to his near approach to the close of his career on earth, and besought him to prepare for that other life which was beyond the grave. He entreated him to employ the balance of his days in repenting of his sins, and in seeking that pardon which God alone can give. In conclusion, Judge Chase said:

"What remains for me is a very necessary but a very painful part of my duty; it is to pronounce that judgment which the law has appointed for crimes of this magnitude. The judgment of the law is, and this Court does award, 'that you be hanged by the neck *until dead ;*' and I pray God Almighty to be merciful to your soul.'"

Samuel Sitgreaves, who conducted the prosecution at the first trial of John Fries, was one of the ablest men Pennsylvania ever produced. He was born in Philadelphia, 1763, where he studied law and was admitted to the bar. He removed to Easton, Northampton county, about 1786, and, by reason of his great abilities immediately took a high position at the bar, and became prominent in politics. His first appearance in public life, was as a member of the Constitutional Convention of Pennsylvania, 1790, in which he took an active part. He was elected to Congress, 1794, and served until 1798. In the impeachment of Senator Blount, of Tennessee, before the United States Senate, he was one of the leading managers, and discharged his duties with great power, talents and fidelity. In 1799 Mr. Sitgreaves went to England as Commissioner under Jay's treaty, and was absent at the time of the second trial of Fries. After the election of Mr. Jefferson he retired from politics and devoted himself to his profession. He became disgusted with the Federalists, but could not affiliate with the Democrats. He spent the balance of his days in retirement.

During the time that John Fries was confined in prison he received much sympathy from the citizens of Philadelphia, and others. Among those, who took deep interest in his fate, was the Rev. Dr. Janeway, an eminent clergymen of that day, who visited him by permission of the authorities, and ministered to him spiritual and other consolation. He presented him a handsome Bible, of duodecimo size, with which to console his hours of confinement. After his sentence to death, May 9, and when he expected shortly to be led to the scaffold for execution, he made a bequest of this Bible to his children, as follows, viz:

"PHILADELPHIA, May 22, 1800."

"MY DEAR CHILDREN.—This Book, presented to me by J. J. Janeway, at his request, I leave as the legacy of your dying father. Let me entreat you to regard it as the best gift of Heaven; as revealing the only way of salvation for lost sinners. I beseech, I command you to read and to study it. I pray that the spirit of God may open your eyes, that you may read it in faith, to the salvation of your immortal souls.

(Signed)     "JOHN FRIES."

The Bible is now in possession of John Fries' descendants, who live in Whitemarsh, Montgomery county, and is cherished by them as a great treasure. The bequest is in his hand writing, and to judge by the language he was by no means an illiterate man. He lived many years after this period, and at his death the sacred volume passed into the hands of those for whom he had intended it.

# The Fries Rebellion.

## CHAPTER XII.

### Pardon of Fries.

The conviction and sentence of Fries increased the excitement already prevailing. The two political parties took up the question of his guilt or innocence and discussed it with great bitterness; the Federalists contending he was guilty of treason and ought to suffer the extreme penalty of the law; the Democrats taking the opposite ground, that he was the victim of tyranny and oppression. The newspapers of that period teem with this violent partizan discussion, and give us an insight into the bitterness that prevailed. When the news spread into the districts where Fries had resisted the execution of the tax law, and it became known, among his neighbors and followers, that he had been condemned to death, the minds of the people were more inflamed than at any past period; and had they possessed the power would undoubtedly have torn him from the hands of the federal government.

There was a strong feeling in favor of Fries, and this increased after his conviction. He was considered a deluded man, who had probably been led astray by other more responsible parties. For this reason, also, there was a desire to save him from execution. This was participated in by both political parties, and an immediate effort was made to obtain a pardon from the President. Fries does not appear to have been actuated by the feeling of a martyr, nor to have had any desire to be distinguished in that way; but was anxious to escape from the unpleasant position in which he found himself. Soon after his sentence, he caused to be presented to the President the following petition:

"PETITION OF JOHN FRIES."

*To the President of the United States:*

"The petition of John Fries respectfully showeth; that your prisoner is one of those deluded and unfortunate men, who, at the Circuit Court of this district, has been convicted of treason against the United States, for which offence he is now under sentence of death. In this awful situation, impressed with a just sense of the crime which he has committed, and with the sincerity of a penitent offender, he entreats mercy and pardon from him on whose determination rests the fate of an unfortunate man. He solicits the interference of the President to save him from an ignominious death, and to rescue a large, and hitherto happy family, from future misery and ruin. If the prayer of his petition should be granted, he will show, by a future course of good conduct, his gratitude to his offended country by a steady and active support of that excellent Constitution and laws, which it has been his misfortune to violate and expose.

(Signed) "JOHN FRIES."
*Philadelphia Prison, May, 1800.*

To the above petition was attached a recommendation, in the following words:

"The subscribers most respectfully recommend the petitioner to the President of the United States. They are warmly attached to the Constitution and laws of their country which they will, on every occasion, and, at every hazard, manifest their zeal to defend and support. But when they reflect on the ignorance, the delusion, and the penitence of the persons involved in the late insurrection, their pity supersedes every vindictive sentiment, and they sincerely think that an exercise of mercy will have a more salutary effect than the punishment of the convicts. It is on this ground that the subscribers, knowing the humanity as well as the fortitude of the President, venture to claim his attention on the present awful occasion, in favor of the wretched father of a numerous family."

In this manner was the application for pardon brought officially before the President for his consideration.

At the time of the first conviction of Fries, Mr. Adams was in Massachusetts, on a visit at Quincy.[1] Colonel Pickering[2] and Mr. Wolcott,[3] two of the members of his Cabinet, immediately wrote him the result of the trial, and expressed their satisfaction at the verdict. The latter mentioned, incidentally, that Mr. Lewis, one of the counsel of the accused, had stated, on all occasions during the trial, that the offence which he had committed did not amount to treason. He also stated that Fries, had frequently said, that "persons of greater conse-

---

[1] Quincy, the home and birth place of the Adamses for several generations, and one of the most beautiful towns of New England, is situated in the township and county of Norfolk, Mass., eight miles S. by E. of Boston. Here were born John Hancock, Josiah Quincy, Jr., and the two Adamses. Quincy is noted for its fine granite quarries, which employ over a thousand workmen, and here the first railroad in America was put in operation, 1826, for the purpose of transporting the granite from its bed to tide water, a distance of three miles. In a stone church, completed in 1828, at a cost of $40,000, is a beautiful marble monument to the memory of John Adams and his wife. Quincy was incorporated in 1792, and the population is about 10,000.

[2] Timothy Pickering was born at Salem, Mass., July 17, 1745, and died there January 29, 1829. He graduated at Harvard, 1763; studied law and admitted to the Bar, 1768. For sometime he was register of deeds, Essex county, and in 1766 was confirmed by Gov. Bernard, lieutenant of militia; in 1775 was elected Colonel, and subsequently joined the Continental Army. In September, 1775, he was commissioned justice of the peace, and two months later, judge of the maritime court for the counties of Suffolk, Essex and Middlesex. He was appointed by Washington Adjutant General to succeed General Reed, and was present at battles of Brandywine and Germantown. In August, 1780, he was appointed Quarter-Master-General of the army to succeed General Nash Greene, who resigned. He was present at the surrender of Yorktown. On leaving the army, 1785, he engaged in business in Philadelphia. In 1787 he removed to the Wyoming Valley, Pa., was a member of the Convention, 1789, to frame the new Constitution. On resignation of General Knox, 1795, he was appointed Secretary of War, and later in the same year, Secretary of State to 1800. He returned to Massachusetts, and in 1802 was appointed President Judge of the Court of Common Pleas; elected U. S. Senate. 1803-1812; member House of Representatives, 1812-16.

[3] Oliver Wolcott was born at Litchfield, Conn., January 11, 1760, and died at New York city, June 1, 1833. He graduated at Yale, 1778, studied law and was admitted to the Bar, 1781. He saw some military service during the Revolution. In 1789 he was appointed Auditor, in 1791 Comptroller, and in 1795 Secretary of Treasury of the United States. He was elected Governor of Connecticut, 1817, and served for 10 years.

sequence had been at the bottom of the business." These letters reached Mr. Adams the evening of May 16, and, the next morning, he answered them. To Mr. Wolcott he wrote as follows:

"QUINCY, May 17, 1799."

"I thank you, sir, for the favor of the 11th, which I received last night. The termination of the trial of Fries, is an important and interesting, and an affecting event. I am unable to conjecture the grounds of Mr. Lewis' opinion and wish I had a sketch of them. Is Fries a native or a foreigner? Is he a man of property and independence, or is he in debt? What has been his previous life? Industrious or idle, sober or temperate?

"It is of importance to discover, if possible, the great man alluded to by Fries, in his observation to Mr. Wood, as at the bottom of the business, and the evidence of any agitation among the insurgents ought to be collected.

"It is of moment, also, to ascertain whether the insurgents had any general view, or extensive communications with others of similar dispositions in other counties or correspondence with other states. We ought also to inquire whether Fries is the most culpable among the guilty, if that can be known. It highly concerns the people of the United States, and especially the federal government, that in the whole progress and ultimate conclusion of this affair, neither humanity be unnecessarily afflicted, nor public justice essentially violated, nor the public safety endangered.

"I have the honor to be, sir, your most obedient and humble servant, (Signed) JOHN ADAMS."

This honest expression of opinion, by Mr. Adams, was not well received by some of the members of his Cabinet, who had marked Fries as a victim to federal power, and they were not well pleased at the prospect of his escaping them, a remote chance of which they thought they could see foreshadowed in the President's letter. In the life of John Adams, by his grandson, Charles Francis Adams, volume 1, page 571, the author thus notices this proceeding: "These letters were received by the persons to whom they were addressed with some dismay. They did not understand why the President should entertain his own views of the law, after the proper Court had adjucated upon it, and they honestly thought that the public safety required an immediate example to be made of Fries. 'Painful as the idea of taking the life of a man,' said Pickering, ' I feel a calm and solid satisfaction that an opportunity is now presented, in executing the just sentence of the law, to crush that spirit, which, if not overthrown and destroyed, may proceed in its career, and overturn the government.' "

Two views were presented when the question of the execution of Fries camp up, but the conflict was postponed for a time, by a new trial being granted.

After the second conviction, and his sentence to death, by Judge Chase, Mr. Adams took the proper measures to inform himself of the probable guilt or innocence of the prisoner, and of such other matters in relation thereto, as would give him a full understanding of the whole case, that he might act justly and fairly in the premises.

There can be no doubt that, at one period, Mr. Adams had determined to let the law take its course, and made up his mind not to interpose the executive clemency. Mr. Hamilton,[4] in his letter on the public conduct of Mr. Adams, states that while the trials were pending, he more than once expressed himself to the effect, "that the accused must found their hopes of escape, either in their innocence, or in the lenity of the juries; since from him, in case of conviction,

---

[4] Alexander Hamilton, one of the ablest Americam statesmen of the early Constitutional era of the United States, was born on the Island of Nevis, West Indies, January 11, 1757, and educated at Columbia College, New York. While a student he organized an artillery company of his fellow students, and took an active part at the battle of Long Island. In January, 1777, he became Washington's Private Secretary and remained with him until April, 1781. He married a daughter of Philip Schuler, 1780. After the War of the Revolution had been fought to a conclusion, the important part he took in the formation, and adoption of the Constitution, and his services in organizing the finances of the new Republic are too well known to need repetition. He fell in a duel with Aaron Burr, July 11, 1804. Alexander Hamilton was one of the most remarkable men that took part in the Revolutionary struggle and the subsequent formation of the Government.

they would have nothing to expect." He further states that
a short time before the pardon he declared that the mistaken
policy of Washington in regard to the Western Insurrection
had been the cause of the second troubles. Whatever the
cause may have been, it is evident his mind had undergone
great change, and that he had come to the determination to
pardon them if he could have justification for doing so. Hence
his anxiety to learn the full particulars of the case, independent of the action of the Court and jury.

Soon after the sentence of death had been pronounced,
Thomas Adams, son of the President, waited upon Mr. Lewis,
one of the counsel of Fries, and told him that his father
wished to know the points and authorities upon which he and
Mr. Dallas had intended to rely in case they had defended
him upon the second trial. The Attorney-General of the
United States made a like request, and, at their solicitation,
Messrs. Dallas and Lewis made a full statement of the points
of the case, which was sent to the President on or before
May 19. About this time a change took place in the
Cabinet, and the President was thus deprived of a portion of
his Constitutional advisers; and when the question again came
up there were only three persons to consult with.

On May 20, he submitted to his Cabinet a series of thirteen questions, which indicate his leaning to the side of
clemency. Mr. Walcott remained firmly of the opinion that
all three of the leaders in the insurrection, Fries, Heaney and
Getman, should be executed, which was called for to inspire
the well disposed with confidence in the government, and the
malevolent with terror. The other ministers believed that
the execution of Fries, alone, would be sufficient to show the
power of the law to punish evil doers; but rather than that
all three should be released, they were in favor of the execution of the whole of them. Mr. Adams appears to have acted
upon his own judgment, and took the responsibility of the
measure without the concurrence of his Cabinet. Having
satisfied his own mind that it was a case in which the executive clemency could be exercised with good effect, and that
the great excitement, prevailing in the country, would be

much more readily allayed by mercy than the opposite course, he determined to grant an unconditional pardon to all the prisoners. For this purpose he caused to be issued the following :

"PROCLAMATION."

"BY JOHN ADAMS, PRESIDENT OF THE UNITED STATES OF AMERICA."

- "PHILADELPHIA, May 23."

"WHEREAS, The late wicked and treasonable insurrection against the just authorities of the United States, of sundry persons in the counties of Northampton, Montgomery and Bucks. in the State of Pennsylvania, in the year 1799, having been speedily suppressed without any of the calamities usually attending rebellion, whereupon peace, order, and submission to the laws of the United States were restored in the aforesaid counties, and the ignorant, misguided and misinformed in the counties have returned to a proper sense of their duty; whereby it is become unnecessary for the public good that any future prosecutions should be commenced or carried on against any person or persons, by reason of their being concerned in the said insurrection ; wherefore be it known that I, John Adams, President of the United States of America, have granted, and by these presents do grant, a full free and absolute pardon, to all and every person or persons concerned in the said insurrection excepting as hereinafter excepted, of all felonies, misdemeanors and other crimes by them respectively done or committed against the United States ; in either of the said counties, before the 12th day of March, in the year 1799 ; excepting and excluding therefrom any person who now standeth indicted or convicted of any treason, misprison of treason, or other offence against the United States; whereby remedying and releasing unto all persons, except as before excepted, all pains and penalties incurred, or supposed to be incurred for, or on account of the premises. Given under my hand and the seal of the United States of America, at the city of Philadelphia, this Twenty-first day of May, in the year of our Lord Eighteen Hundred, and of the Independence of the said United States, the twenty-fourth. (Signed) "JOHN ADAMS."

This proclamation, as will be noticed, did not embrace the cases of Fries, Heany and Getman, already under sentence, and a special pardon was made out for them a few days afterward, which struck the fetters from their limbs and set them free. The biographer of John Adams states that "the Cabinet had been consulted at every step, but nevertheless, when the President ordered the pardons made out the next day, for all the offenders, the disaffected members viewed the Act with disappointment, and Mr. Adams was charged with inconsistency, and having been governed by personal motives for the Act. It was said to be a 'fatal concession to his enemies,' as the Act was 'popular in Pennsylvania.' Such was the tone of the disappointed Federalists who saw in it another departure from the policy they would have introduced into the federal government."

# The Fries Rebellion.

## CHAPTER XIII.

### Conclusion.

The action of President Adams, in pardoning Fries, Haney and Getman, was the cause of much dissention in the Cabinet, and, between him and his political friends, it engendered a bitterness of feeling that was never entirely obliterated. So far as official action was concerned, the act of pardon closed the drama of the "Rebellion," and removed it from further consideration. This final disposition of the affair, however, did not have the effect of taking it out of politics, but, for a number of years afterward, it was made a standing text, particularly in eastern Pennsylvania, for philipics against the Federal party. In the campaign which soon followed, between Mr. Jefferson[1] and John Adams, it was used with tremendous effect against the latter, and assisted very materially in hurling him and his friends from power. It was one of the leading causes which produced the great political revolution

---

[1] Thomas Jefferson, third President of the United States, was born April 3, 1743, at Shadwell, Abermarle county, Virginia. He was graduated from Williams' and Mary's College, 1762, and at that early day was noted for his scholarship in languages. He studied law with George Wythe, then at the head of the Virginia Bar, in whom he found a friend through life, and was admitted to the Bar, 1767. He would have made a great lawyer had he continued in the profession, but he naturally inclined to politics. He was elected to the House of Burgesses, 1768, and continued a member until it was closed by the Revolution. When the oppression of Parliament led the colonies to throw off the yoke of Great Britain, Jefferson threw himself into the contest with all his vigor and zeal. We need not recount his subsequent distinguished career. The authorship of the Declaration of Independence, if he had done nothing else, would make his name immortal.

in this State in 1800, and the Federal party never recovered from the odium it entailed upon it. We remember when the names of Fries, Haney and Getman were mingled in our local county politics; and more than one Democrat, in Bucks county, owed his elevation to office to the skillful use made of the events growing out of the house-tax law of 1798.

The part Mr. Adams took, in the matter of pardoning the insurgents, was alike creditable to his head and heart, and tends to remove, in some degree, the stigma his approval of the Alien and Sedition law, and the House Tax fastened upon his Administration. That he was moved to it by the best of motives, and prompted by the dictates of a kind heart, there can be no question, and it is equally certain the Act was his own, and against the wish and advice of his Cabinet. He has left behind him a record of the satisfaction it gave him. In his tenth letter, in the Boston *Patriot*, of May 17, 1809, remarking on his responsibility for all his executive acts, and that it was his right and duty to be governed by his own judgment, although in direct conflict with the advice of all his ministers, he says: " This was my situation in more than one instance It had been so in the nomination of Mr. Gerry; it was afterwards so in the pardon of Fries; two measures that I recollect with infinite satisfaction, and which will console me in my last hour."

It was suspected at the time of the disturbance, that more prominent men than the unfortunates who fell into the hands of the Federal authorities were at the bottom of the rebellion; and even the names of some of the leaders of the Federal party were connected with it. After the trial, John Fries told a Mr. Wood, a clerk in one of the Departments, and who was also clerk of the prison, " that *great men* were at the bottom of this business." Oliver Wolcott, in a letter to John Adams, dated Philadelphia, May 11, 1799, states that B. McClerachan, a member of the Assembly of Pennsylvania, was certainly an agitator among the insurgents. One authority upon the subject says :

" Much of the blame attending upon this disturbance is cast

upon Mr. Sitgreaves, formerly a member of Congress from the Bucks district, and Eyerly, both disappointed politicians. The former followed the march of the troops and appears to have been busy in hunting up persons who had opposed the law. Eyerly was defeated at the election that fall. Fries was a Federalist, and ardent supporter of John Adams' administration, on which account it is supposed he was not afraid of an arrest, believing that his Federal friends would not molest him. Probably Sitgreaves and Eyerly are those to whom Fries refers, that more prominent men were at the bottom of it. It is hinted that they were at the bottom of it and left Fries in the lurch. This is given as the reason that the Federal members of the Legislature opposed the institution of any inquiry into the cause of the disturbance. It is said it was the desire of the Federalists to bring odium on the Republicans by ordering federal troops into the county to put down the rebellion."

However this may be—we mean the participation of men of prominence in the disturbance, we think the matter is now pretty clearly established, that the affair had given to it much greater importance than it merited. We are also well convinced, had the proper steps been taken to quiet the agitation, through the agency of the local authorities there would never have been any need of the interposition of the Federal authorities. In his opinion we are sustained by some of the actors in the scenes that grew out of it. Among others, an officer of the army, writing from camp, while it lay in Bucks county, says: " I need not add after what I have before written to you, that every hour's experience confirms me more and more that this expedition was not only unnecessary, but violently absurd. I can take upon me to assert, that excepting in the rash act of rescuing the people under arrest from the Marshall, there has not been even a desire of resistance manifested, and the most marked censure of many persons now in custody. I do verily believe that a sergeant and six men might have performed all the service for which we have been assembled at so heavy an expense to the United States, and with such a loss of important time to us, especially those who are in the mercantile line."

This seems to have been the opinion of all who were acquainted with the whole affair, except those violent partisans whose prejudices were too strong and too bitter to permit them to judge the case with fairness. The whole cost of the expedition to the United States is said to have been $80,000.

When Fries was liberated there was great rejoicing throughout the country, but the anti-Federalists failed to give Mr. Adams credit for his act of mercy and clemency. As would naturally be the case, they attributed the act, which he said "would console him in his last hours," to sinister motives, and, if anything, they increased the bitterness of their attack upon him and his administration. Such, however, is the history of political parties the world over, and we are not surprised to find no departure therefrom in the exciting times of '98 and '99.

The subsequent history of Fries is brief and void of interest. Upon his release from imprisonment he went directly to the humble home which had sheltered him before he became so famous, and again entered into the ordinary current of life. He resumed his old avocation of vendue crying, and, as before, in company with his little dog traversed the county back and forth, crying the sales of his neighbors and acquaintance. The events of the " Rebellion" left some bitterness behind it took years to heal, and, from time to time, this lingering ill-feeling broke out in that section of the county. There was much hostility against Penrose, who piloted the troops to Bunker Hill when they captured Fries, and the friends of the latter hardly ever forgave him. A few years after his return home Conrad Marks and his friends came down to Quakertown to whip Penrose, who, with a number of his neighbors, was breaking the roads filled with snow drifts. Marks mistook his man, got hold of a nephew of the one he sought and received a good whipping for his trouble. It is also related that soon after his pardon the friends of Fries, who lived near Sumneytown, Montgomery county, raised a Liberty Pole, rather as a mark of exultation over the defeat of the schemes

of the Federalists. John Rodrock, the same who had received indignity at the hands of Fries, was in Philadelphia at the time attending market, and, on his return sent his hired man to cut the pole down, which he accomplished. The people soon got wind of it and pursued and caught the party before they had crossed the line into Bucks. They placed some penalty upon them, but the nature of it we have not learned.²

In a previous chapter we mentioned that John Fries had done his country some service during the Revolutionary War. At that time he was living at Charlestown, Milford township. He was in active service during the war. Between these periods, and while spending some time at home, he was the hero of a spirited affair. While the enemy occupied Philadelphia a party of British light horse, on a foraging expedition in the upper end of Bucks county, were returning to the city through Charlestown in the night. His wife hearing the clatter of hoofs, got up and looked out of the window just before daylight, and saw the troopers marching by with a large number of cattle in charge. She said to her husband, "Why, John here goes a troop of Light Horse all dressed in red; and I guess they must be the British." Fries got up immediately and dressed, and went first to the houses of Hoover and Wykert, near neighbors, whom he awoke and informed of what was going on. He then went around the neighborhood and aroused the people whom he headed and, with them, went in pursuit of the retreating British. They overtook the soldiers near the Spring House tavern, and compelled them to relinquish the cattle and hasten their march to Philadelphia. The cattle were driven back and returned to their owners.

John Fries continued to reside in Milford township to the

---

² The war on "Liberty Poles," made by the Federalists of 1800, is verified by several persons. Jesse Nace, Philadelphia, writes us as follows on the subject, while this volume was being prepared for the press: "Your story of the unwritten history of Bucks county, read before the Historical Society of Penna., and printed in the Philadelphia *Times*, revived in my mind, the sayings of my father, Henry Nace, who participated in that event, that the people had erected 'Liberty Poles' and the soldiers (light horsemen) cut them down. I saw no illusion in your address to this fact, and if father were correct, this addition to your paper would substantially strengthen it. Father was born in Tinicum, March, 1777, consequently he was 22 years old when the occurrences of 1798-99 took place. He said his first vote was for Jefferson for President.'"

day of his death, which took place in 1818.[2] He was buried in the grave-yard at Charlestown, where his remains now lie, without a stone to mark their resting-place. The allegation that Fries opened a tin store in Philadelphia after his pardon is wholly without foundation. Such a statement is found in a note at the conclusion of the published account of the trial, and was probably inserted there on some rumor which prevailed at that day, without the author taking the trouble to satisfy himself of its truth. When we visited his son Daniel, we questioned him, particularly upon this point, and he assured us that his father returned to Milford township, where he continued to follow his old occupation to the day of his death. The same was stated to us by some of the old residents of Quakertown, who knew him well in their younger days. At his decease, his son Daniel assumed the occupation of a vendue cryer, which he followed until he removed to near Sumneytown, where he now resides at the age of nearly 80 years.* Another son, Solmon, lived at Whitemarsh, and both of them left numerous descendants. The father of John Fries, whose name was Simon, came from Wales, and first settled in Maryland, but afterward removed to Montgomery county, in this State, where he died.

We now conclude this historic episode of Bucks county, and take leave of the reader. In writing the preceding account of the "Fries Rebellion" we were influenced by two considerations; the first a desire to give a correct account of what was an important affair in its day, and hitherto but imperfectly understood; the second, a desire to do justice to

---

[2] From an examination of the register's office at Doylestown, Bucks county, it appears John Fries died about the last of February, 1818, at the age of 70. His will is dated June 6, 1815, and probated March 1, 1818. At the time of his death he lived in Lower Milford township, Bucks county. His two sons, John and Solomon, were his executors. The will mentions two pieces of real estate, a lot of 14 acres in Lower Milford, and one of 3 acres in Marlborough township, Montgomery county. The names of his surviving children given in the will, are Solomon, John, Daniel, Sarah, Margaret and Catharine. The wife's name was Margaret. After paying his debts and funeral expenses the residue of this estate was divided among his children, "share and share alike." As we have been unable to find the settlement of his estate, we are ignorant of its amount.

---

* 1858.

those who played the leading parts. If we have succeeded in one, or both desires, we have accomplished our purpose.

Of John Fries we have formed a more favorable opinion than we entertained when we commenced writing. We believe him to have been an earnest and honest, but misguided man, who was moved to the course he took by what he considered his duty. The conduct of Mr. Adams shows him to have been actuated by a sense of duty, as he understood it. and the pardon of the "insurgents" rescues his memory from some of the charges brought against him. He was, no doubt, influenced to some extent, by the high political excitement of the day, but he cannot justly be accused of cruelty in the share he had in the troubles of the period. All the actors in these scenes have long since passed beyond the bar of public opinion, and their acts should now be judged with fairness and candor from the standpoint of History, whose chiefest honor is impartiality.

[THE END.]

# APPENDIX.

# The Fries Rebellion.

### Jacob Rice's Letter.

The following letter, written by the late Jacob Rice, of Bethlehem, Pa., to the late John W. Jordan, of the Historical Society of Pennsylvania, under date of April 6, 1860, is of interest in connection with the subject matter of this volume. As he was conversant with the outbreak, and the causes leading up to it, his opinion is entitled to weight:

"The assertion made by John Fries, that 'great men were at the bottom of this business,' was no doubt correct, and it would not be very difficult, at this late day, to point out the names of some of the individuals to whom he alluded. Mr. Davis' inference in this matter, so far as the late Messrs. Sitgreaves and Eyerly are supposed to be concerned, is, to my certain knowledge, entirely erroneous, and I much regret that he has, no doubt, unintentionally placed their characters in a false position, which they do not deserve. This unfortunate affair happened at a period of great political excitement, and I do not believe that a strictly impartial history can at this time be furnished. The sources from which Mr. Davis has drawn this information appear to me to have been too favorable to the party opposing the measures of the United States Government, as much of the blame, according to his statement, is laid to the charge of the Assessors, etc., which may be correct as it regards Bucks county. In Northampton county such a charge cannot be sustained, Mr. Eyerly having selected the best, most discreet and honorable men to be found in his district as his assistants. The rebellion was mainly confined to the township of Milford, in Bucks, and the townships of

Upper and Lower Milford and Salisbury, in Northampton, now Lehigh county. There was much dissatisfaction with the tax law in the townships north and west of the Lehigh, yet I do not know of a single armed man that came to the rescue from any point north of the Lehigh river.

"My impression has always been that if Colonel Nichols had not given up his prisoners, Bethlehem would have been burned and razed to the ground. Such were the threats which induced Joseph Horsfield and others to prevail on the Marshal to yield."

# The Fries Rebellion.

### Last Will and Testament of John Fries.

In the name of God Amen, I, John Fries, of Lower Milford township, in the county of Bucks, State of Pennsylvania, Yeoman, though reduced to a low state of bodily strength, yet being of sound mind, memory and understanding, (blessed be Almighty God for the same) and considering the uncertainty of transitory life, think it necessary to dispose of those worldly goods that God, in mercy, hath given me to enjoy, by this, my last will and testament, in a manner hereafter expressed, that is to say, first of all, I will that all my just debts and funeral expenses be well and truly paid by my executors, hereafter named, as soon after my decease as conveniently may be, and that as soon as possible a true inventory and appraisement may be taken of all my movables and effects, outstanding debts and further personal property, which said effects and property together, with my real estate (except those goods taken by my wife) I do order and direct my executors to sell and dispose by public vendue, as quick as possible, after my decease, as may be convenient:

*Item:* I give and bequeath unto my loving wife Margaret one bed and bedding, one chest, one table and such other goods as my executors may think necessary for her own use. I also give and bequeath to my said wife forty dollars yearly, during her natural life, which is to be paid to her by my executors out of my estate yearly and every year as long as she may live, and in case there should not be enough for her maintainance, my will is that my said wife shall have as much of my estate as is necessary for her support. *Item:* I give and bequeath unto my grandson, Samuel, (a lad that now lives with me) the just and full sum of forty dollars gold and silver money, to be paid to a guardian (whom I shall hereafter appoint) in one year after my departure. *Item:* I give and bequeath to my two other grandchildren, the heirs of my daughter Catharine, deceased, (the late wife of George Gable) one share of my estate their mother would have become heir to, if she had been living) to be paid to their guardian (whom I shall appoint) at a convenient time for making the division of my estate. *Item:* I nominate and appoint my trusty friend, Jacob Loh, of Lower Milford township aforesaid, sole guardian of these three minor children above mentioned, whom I request to receive the money as above willed and to put the same on interest in good safe hands, and to pay the said minors severally as they arrive to the age of twenty-one years. *Item:* I nominate and appoint my two sons, Solomon and John Fries, co-executors of this my last will and testament, giving them full power and absolute authority to sell and dispose of the lot whereon I live, situated in Lower Milford aforesaid, containing fourteen acres, (be the same more or less) with all the buildings and appurtenances thereunto belonging, or in any wise appertaining, and another lot, situated in Marlborough township, Montgomery county, containing three acres of land (be it more or less) giving them full power and absolute authority to make and execute good and firm titles, good and effective conveyances in law on the same unto such person, or persons that may or shall purchase the same, and unto his or their heirs and assigns forever, as I myself might, or could, do were I living, and that as soon after my decease as may be convenient, and the money arising from the said sales, as well as from my personal estate that may be remaining after my just debts are paid and legacies aforesaid. *Item:* I give and bequeath unto my seven children, to wit, Solomon, John, Daniel, Elizabeth, Sarah, Margaret and Catharine, to be equally divided between them, share and share alike, but the share of my daughter Catharine, who has departed this life, is to be paid to her two children, or their guardian, as above directed. Finally, I do revoke, annul, and make void all former and other wills by me heretofore made or declared to be made, either by word of mouth or in writing, ratifying and confirming this only written, on both sides of this sheet of paper to be my last. In witness whereof, I have hereunto set my hand and seal the sixth day of June, in the year of our Lord one thousand eight hundred and fifteen.

     (Signed)   JOHN FRIES. [SEAL.]

Signed, sealed and acknowledged by the testator, as his last will and testament, in the presence of us, the hereunto subscribed witnesses, who, at his request, have set our names, Morgan Custard, Wm. Getman, Bucks county, Pa., on the 9th day of March 1818.

William Getman, one of the subscribing witnesses to the foregoing writing, purporting to be the last will and testament of John Fries, deceased, appeared before me, and on this solemn affirmation, taken and subscribed, did declare and say that he was present and saw John Fries, the testator, sign, seal and acknowledge the same to be his last will and testament, and that, at the time of his so doing, he was of sound mind and memory, and of deposing, understanding, as he, this affirment believed, and, that at the same time, this affirment saw Morgan Custard, the other subscribing witness, sign his name as a witness, at the request and in the presence of the testator, and further that the name William Getman above is of his, this affirment's own proper handwriting, and further saith not. William Getman, affirmed and subscribed before me, day and date above.

    (Signed)   JOHN PUGH, Register.

*Bucks County ss.* Be it remembered, that on the 9th of March, 1818, the foregoing last will and testament of John Fries was duly proven, when letters testamentary thereof were granted unto Soloman Fries and John Fries, the executors therein named, they having first been duly sworn, well and truly to administer the same. Witness my hand and seal of office. (Signed)  JOHN PUGH, Register.

# INDEX.

## A

Adams, John, 3, 7, 29, 70, 71, 115; to Wolcott, 132, 12, 14, 17, 133, 137; Action Creditable, 138; Informs Himself, 133; Acted on his Own Judgment, 134; Adams' Administration of, 4, 11.
Adams, Charles Francis, 132.
Adams, Thomas, 134.
Administration, 14.
*Advertiser*, The Daily, 80, 92.
*Adler*, Reading, 112.
Allentown, Commissioners Meet at, 39; The Army Marches to, 111.
Army, Continental, 1, 10.
Army, Federal, 82.
Army, Review of, 108.
Artman, Henry, 72.
Artillery, U. S., 81.
Arrests Made, Number and Names, 104.
Army Officer, Letter from, 139.
Authorities, Federal, 55, 69, 72.
Assessors, 3, 6, 17, 20; Assessors Give up Assessments, 35.
Assessment Rates of, 3.
Assessments, 16.

## B

Balliott, 21, 39; at Trexlertown Meeting, 45.
Balliott, Colonel, 48.
Balliott, Mr., 59, 72.
Barnett, William, 59, 61.
Barnett, John, 59.
Barnett, William, 62.
Baker, Dr., 68.
Baynton, Adjutant-General Peter, 76, 77; Issues Order for Troops, 77.
Bethlehem, Marshal Returned to, 48; 50, 51, 53, 54, 55.
Bethlehem, South, 56, 57
Bethlehem, 53, 57, 58, 59, 60, 61, 62, 67, 69, 72.
Bridge, Lehigh, 6.
Brunner, Margaret, 8.
Brunner, David, 8.
Brandywine, 53.
Brown, General, 59.
Bucks, 69, 72.
Blues, Macpherson, 78.
Bristol, Troops Ordered to, 78.
Bucks County, Troops from, 77, 113.
Bunker Hill, 93.

## C

Camp Hill, 10.
Cavalry, Troops, 76.
Carlisle, 79.
Cabinet, Changes in, 134.
Campaign, Cost of, 140.
Chase, Judge, Warrants Returnable to, 47; Conduct of, 124; Addresses Fries, 126, 133
Chapman, Seth, 5.
Chapman, James, 6, 16, 17, 19, 21, 22, 22, 25, 26, 27 105; Sketch of, 106, 107.
Charlestown, 9, 12, 15.
Childs, Cephas, 6, 22, 16, 25, 26, 27, 28, 29, 30, 31, 32, 33; Threatened by Insurgents, 31.
Clark, Samuel, 6, 16, 17, 19, 25, 26, 22, 68.
Court, U. S., 20, 32.
Cline, John, 57.
Congress, 2; Act of, July 9, 1798, 3, 3, 4, 15, 21, 27; Power to Lay Taxes, 83.
Commissioners, 5, 6.
Company, Captain Mosher's, 80.
Contingent, Northampton, 57.
Constitution, The, 70.
County, Bucks, 2, 5, 7, 8, 13, 16, 54, 67, 73, 75, 76, 82.
County, Northampton, 2, 4, 5, 7, 12, 13, 34, 40, 48, 51, 54, 62, 69, 70, 72, 73, 75, 75, 76, 77, 82, 113.
County, Montgomery, 45, 8, 16, 26, 69, 73; Troops from, 77, 75, 76, 81, 82.
County, Berks, 4, 5.
County, Wayne, 5.
County, Lehigh, 51.
County, Luzerne, 5.
County, Lancaster, 75.
County, Cumberland, Cavalry Ordered from, 78.
Contingent, Northampton, 61, 62.
Colonies, American, 9.
Crooked Billet, 10.
Cortez, 97.
Creek, Boggy, 8, 9.
Creek, Swamp, 97.

## D

Davidson, Samuel, 5.
Davis, 68.
Dallas, Alex. J., 117; Dallas' Defence of Fries, 121; Dallas' and Lewis,' Statement of Fries' Case, 134; Withdraw, 134.
Democracy, 2c.
Delaware, The, 51, 53.
DeKalbe, Baron, 53.
Dixon, Mr., 60.
Districts, German, Inhabitants of, 105.
Dogs, Homer's Hero's, 97.
Dunlap, Captain, 77.

## E

Easton, 42, 59.
Eberhart, Sent to Philadelphia, 99.
Edwards, Caleb, 9, 94.
Edwards, William, 9, 93.
Edmonds, Mr., 13.
Edwards, Jacob E., 3.
Edwards, Samuel, 95.
Elliott, Captain, 51.
Emaus, 48, 66.
English, The, 28.
Erdman, Interpreter for Witnesses, 119.
Europe, 2.
Eyerley, Jacob, 5, 21, 42; Appointed Commissioners, Northampton, 38; Divides Township, 39; Explains the Law. 43; Reads Petition, 44, 48, 59, 64, 65.
Eyerley, Daniel, 51.
Eyerman, Accompanies Marshal to Make Arrests, 48, 49, 59; Clergyman, 100.

## F

Federalists, 61.
Federalists, Anti, 61.
Foulke, Everhard, 6, 19, 21, 22, 25, 27, 28.
Frantz, Zeno, 29.
Foulke and Rodrock, Messrs., 30.
Foulke, 31, 32.
Frailey, Colonel, 113.
Foulke, Everhard, 121.
Fox, John, 6.
France, 2, 26.
French, 2.
Fries, John, 2, 7, 8, 9; Children of, 9, 11, 12, 13, 14, 15, 17, 18, 19, 20, 21, 25, 26, 27, 27, 28, 29, 30, 31, 34, 32, 54, 57, 62, 63; Captain, 64, 64, 65, 66, 67, 68, 71, 72; Military Called for, 75, 93; First Object of Capture, 93; Macpherson, Head of, 93; Arrests of, 94; Two Accounts of Capture. 95; Fries' Dog, Account of, 96; Examination of, 98, 99; Sent to Philadelphia, 99; Betrayed by his Dog, 97; Trial of, 115; Indictment of 116; Motion Argued, 118; Sitgreaves Opens Case, 119; Names of Jurors, 119; Pleads Not Guilty, 119; Witnesses, 120; Confession of, read, 120; New Trial Granted to, 123; Sentence Imposed on, 126; Letter to his Children, 127; Bible Presented to, 127; Verdict Against, 122; Sympathy for, 127; Stroug Feeling in Favor of, 129; Conviction and Sentence of, 129; Movement for Pardon of, 129; Petition for Pardon, 130; Pickering Favored Execution of, 133; Heaney and Getman, Pardon of, 136; Pardon of, Engendered Bad Feeling and Entered Politics, 137; A Federalists, 139; Subsequent History of, 140; Recovers Cattle from British, 141; Release Well Received, 141; Death of, 142; Character of, 143.
Fries, Daniel, 8; 14, 57; Tried to Capture, 97; Death of, 98, 142.
Fries, Jacob, 22, 23, 27, 31.
Fries, Solomon, 142.

## G

Galloway, Joseph, 8.
Germans, 2, 28, 67.
Gerry, Mr., 138.
Getman, 7. 12, 13, 137, 138.
Green, Richard, 30.
Greenmeyer, 111.
Government, The, 20, 61.
Governor, Message of the, 73; To Make due Inquiry, 74.
Graber, James, 17.
Grant, Thomas, Jr., 5.
Great Britain, 9.
Griffith, Esquire, 32.
Griffith, Mrs., 32.

## H

Hager, Christian, 12.
Hagersville, 12.
Heaney, Frederick, 7, 12; Children of, 13, 71, 137, 138.
Heaney, George, 12.
Heister, Colonel, 113.
Heckewelder, 44.
Heller, Meeting at House of, 42.
Henry, William, 43.
Henry, Judge, Attends Meeting at Hellers', 43; Issued Subpœnas, 45, 46, 59, 65.
Henry, Capt. John, 79; Hamilton, Views of, 133.
Harper, Robert Goodloe, 92.

Hartman, Herman, 51.
Hartzell, Isaac, 61.
Helmuth, Rev. Chas. Henry, Address of, 87.
House-Tax, Insurgents Dam the, 33.
House, Jacob Fries, 28.
House, Sisters', 53.
House, The Question Referred, 74.
House, Spring, 81.
Horsfield, Mr., 59, 64, 65.
Hotel, Eagle, 51.
Horne, Assessor, 39.
Hoover's, John and Jacob, 31, 17, 18, 68.

## I

Iden, James C., Letter of, 41.
Indians, Mohican, 53.
Inhabitants, Distress of, 110.
Insurgents, The, 73; Persued by Troops, 105; Arrested, 106.
Insurrection, Western, 73, 134.
Insurrection, Whiskey, 1, 10
Iredell, Judge, 115; Charge to Grand Jury, 116, 118.
Irvine, Captain, 73.

## J

Jamison, John, 31, 67, 68, 121.
Janeway, Rev. Dr., 127.
Jarrett, Captain, 55, 64, 68.
Jenkinson, Isaac, 5.
Jury, Case Given to, 122.
Jurors, Names of, 124.

## K

Kachline, John, 94.
Karackerstown, Fourteen Surrender at, 111.
Kearne Mr. 40.
Kennedy, Captain, 77.
Klein, John, 15.
Klein, Jacob, 19.
Kline George, 68.
Kuyder, Capt , 16, 23, 29, 31.

## L

Lacey, Gen. John, 10.
LaFayette, 53.
Liberty, 21; Pole Cut Down, 110; War on, 141.
Laws, Alien and Sedition, 3, 4, 36, 41, 138.
Law, House Tax, 4.
Lesher, Captain, 77.
Leiper, Captain, 77, 113.
Lancaster, Joseph R., 32.
Lancaster, 79.
Levering, Abraham, 65, 70.
Legislature, The, 75.
Lewistown, 18.
Lee, Henry, 2.
Lee's Division, 53.
Lewis, Mr., 131.
Light Horse, Lancaster, 112.

## M

Macpherson, General, 8; Brigadier-General, 76; Designated to Command Troops, 77; Appointed Brigadier U. S. A., 78, 81; Address of, 82; Forewarns People, 86; Address of, 87; Probably Marched with Cavalry, 92, 112, 113.
Marks, Conrad, 30, 21, 34, 54, 57, 67, 68, 71; Surrendered, 108.
Marks, John, 50
Massachusetts, 1.
Marshal United States, 50, 54, 58, 59, 60, 62,

63, 64, 69, 70; Armed Force to be Sent With, 90.
Meadow, Smith's, 97.
Milford, Upper and Lower, 26, 68, 17, 19, 22, 54.
Mifflin, Governor, 73, 76, 80
Montgomery, Captain, 77, 112, 113.
Morrell, Captain, 77.
Melbecke, Lieutenant, 108.
Moravians, 51.
Moore, Richard, 100.
Mulhallon, John, 61.
Mitchell, George, 15, 17, 17, 19, 19, 21, 71.
Mill, Mathers', 8.
Mill, Stover's, 12
Mill, Hoover's, 20.
Millarstown, 49, 54, 57, 61, 62, 72; Troops March for, 100; Army Encamped at, 108.
Michael, Nicholas, 41, 42.
Military Force Called for, 73.
Militia, Requisition from, 75.
Mount Vernon, 3.
McHenry, James, 76.
McClerachan B., An Agitator, 138.
Moretz, At Meeting, 44.

## N

Nazareth, 48, 51.
Nanticokes, 52.
Nace, Enos, P., 97.
Newtown, Troops Rendezvous at, 78; Troops reach, 79.
New York, Troops Leave, 78; Troops March from, 79.
New Jersey, Requisition for Malitia on, 80.
Nichols, Colonel, 50, 64; Marshal Makes Arrests, 48, 70.
Nitschman, David, 51.
Northampton, Opposition to Law in, 38.

## O

Officers, Letters About, 95, 109.

## P

Pardon, Recommendations for, 130; Proclamation of, 135; Cabinet Divided on, 136; Proclamation of, 136.
Patriot, Boston, 138.
Penrose, Daniel, 31; Penrose, David, 93.
Pennsylvania, 1, 4, 5; The State of 99; The Governor of 73; The State of, 75.
Peters, Judge, Deposition Sent to, 46; Examine Witnesses, 46, 46.
Peters, Judge, 54, 69, 72; John Fries Examined Before, 98; Called as Witness, 120.
Pheister, George L., 22.
Philadelphia, 7, 18; The Marshal Leaves to Serve Subpœnas, 48, 59, 62, 64, 65, 72, 73; The Troops Leave, 81, 81; Prisoners in Jail at, 113.
Pickering, Timothy, 71; The Views of, 133.
Politics, The Condition of, 36; The Influence of, 109.
Porter, James M., Recollections of, 123.
Posse, The Marshal's, 63, 64, 65.
Pottery, Penrose's, 100.
President, The, 3, 4; He Issues a Proclamation, 69, 69.
Proclamation, The President, 72, 73.
President, The and Cabinet, 4.
Pulaski, Count, 53.
Porter and Wharton, Captains, Search for Fries, 93.

## Q

Quakertown, 9, 13, 22, 23, 29, 30, 32; What Took Place, 35, 93, 97; Army Encamped at 100, 108; The Army Leaves, 108; Quincy, Mr. Adams at, 131.

## R

Rawle, William, 117.
Rawle and Sitgreaves, 118.
Rebellion, Fries, 2, 13; The a National Affair, 73, 75; Fries, a Factor at Jefferson's Election, 137; Great Men at Bottom of, 138. Cost of, 140; Shays', 1; Shays', 73.
Revolution, The, 1, 53.
Reed, Collinson, 5.
Railroad, The North Pennsylvania, 92.
Reading, 5; Troops March to, 111; Troops March from, 112; Outrage at, 112.
Ritter, Martin, 55.
River, Lehigh, 57, 61.
Road, Ridge, 81; The Old Bethlehem, 91, 97.
Roberts, Israel, 17, 20, 21, 71, 121.
Roberts, Daniel, 68.
Rodrock, John, 6, 16, 17, 22, 28, 31 33.
Rodrock and Foulke, 32.
Rodman, Lieutenant, W. M., 78.
Roberts, Enoch, 35.
Roths, Christian, 59, 61.
Rocks, The, 100.

## S

Savannah, 53.
Sacket, Alfred, 18.
Schmyser Michael, 5.
Schaeffer, George, 44, 49.
Schymer, John, 44
Schlaugh, Philip, 59, 65.
Schlichter, Andrew, The Farm of, 92.
Schneider, Jacob, 112.
Sellersville, 13; The Present, 92.
Schneider, Jacob, 113.
Sentinel, Bull Shot by, 111
Shawnese, 52.
Shankwyler, 49, 50, 72, 60.
Shays' Daniel, 1.
Shoemaker, Captain, 79.
Shewell, Nathaniel, 107.
Shiffert, Andrew, 55.
Sims, Captain, 77, 78.
Singmaster, 18, 29, 30, 77.
Sitgreaves, U. S. Attorney, 42; U. S. District Attorney, Draws up Form of Warrant, 46; 125, 139.
Smith, Peter, 29.
Snyder, Mr., 48, 39.
Spangenberg, Bishop, 52.
Spring House, Headquarters at, 82.
Store, Rufe's, 18.
Staeler, Captain, 62
Stephen, Adam, 51, 72.
Spinnerstown, 17; 9.
Sumneytown, 98.
Swartz, Daniel.

## T

Tax, Direct, Passed, 3; On What Laid, 83; Rates of, 84; Law, Unpopularity of, 37.
Tavern, Rodrock's, 18.
Tavern, Jacob Fries', 27, 25, 26, 27, 29, 123.
Tavern, Knoch, Roberts, 29, 31.
Tavern, Sellers', 30; Troops March from, 99, 91.
Tavern, Mitchell's, 27, 68, 71.
The Spring House, 91.
Tavern, Gennes, 55.
Tavern, Gary's, 15.
Tavern, Ritter's, 57, 60.
Tavern, Conrad Marks', 62.
Taylor, Captain, 77.

Tavern, The Sun, 58, 60, 62.
Tanyard, Lester's, 97.
Terror, System of, 102, 103.
Trenton, Troops Reach, 79.
Trail, Judge, 42.
Treasury, Secretary of, 4, 5, 21.
Thomas William, 23.
Thomas, Samuel, 97.
Thomas, Edward, 97.
Trexlertown, Meeting at, 45 ; Captain Jarrett's Company at, 45.
Trumbower, Chased by Soldiers, 94.
Trumbauersville, 17, 22, 23, 26.
Township, Milford, 8, 7, 6, 12, 12, 14, 16, 25, 29, 32, 67, 71.
Township, Rockhill, 12, 13, 92.
Township, Tinicum, 18.
Township Richland, 6, 6, 97.
Township, Hatfield, 8.
Township, Plumstead, 6.
Township, Plainfield, 12, 13.
Township, Bushkill, 13.
Township, Weisenburg, 40.
Township, Lynn, 40.
Township, Lehigh, 59 ; Twelve Arrested in, 48.
Township, Hamilton, 40, 41.
Township, Upper Milford, 40 ; Meeting in, 43.
Township, Chestnut Hill, 39.
Township, Moore, 40.

Township, Penn, 40.
Township, Low Hill, 40.
Township, Heidelburg, 40.
Troops, American, 53.
Troops, Regular, Ordered Out, 78.
Troops March, 80; Instructions for, 80 ; March for Quakertown, 99 ; March from Sellers' Tavern, 100 ; Alarmed, 106 ; Excesses Committed by, 109 ; Their Presence Inspires Terror, 100.

## U

United States, The, 26, 69, 70, 60, 71 ; The Laws of the, 61, 75, 82 ; The Seal of the, 71 ; Interest of the, 74 ; The Officers of the, 69 ; The President of the, 70, 73, 82.

## V

Valley, Wyoming, 52.
VanBuskirk, 49.
Verdict Rendered, 125.
Virginia, 3, 21.

## W

Washington, 2, 3, 10 ; Mistaken Policy of, 13 ; 53.
Wells, Isaiah, 123.
Whigs and Tories, 103.
Wheeler, Israel, 5.
Whiskey, 11.
Witnesses Called, 121.
Wiedner, Daniel, 26.
Wiedner, 27.
Winters, Christopher, 59.
Williams, Lieutenant, John, 80.
Whitemarsh, 8, 10, 142.
Wolcott, Oliver, 138 ; Favors Execution, 134
Woolstencraft, Lieutenant, 79.
Wood, Mr., 138 ; Fries' Observation to, 134.
Wyker, Reuben L., 18.
Wyker, George, 18.
Wyker, Nicholas, 18.

## Z

Zellers, 30, 30.
Zeigler, George I., 25, 26.
Zantzenger, Paul 5.
Zinzendorf, Count, 52, 53.

www.ingramcontent.com/pod-product-compliance
Lightning Source LLC
Chambersburg PA
CBHW020842160426
43192CB00007B/753